A JOURNEY TO GOD

A JOURNEY TO GOD

REFLECTIONS ON THE HIKAM OF IBN ATA'ILLAH

Jasser Auda

PUBLISHED BY THE PRESS SYNDICATE OF AWAKENING PUBLICATIONS
Uplands Business Centre, Bernard Street, Swansea, SA2 0DR, United Kingdom

AWAKENING PUBLICATIONS
Uplands Business Centre, Bernard Street, Swansea, SA2 0DR, United Kingdom
P.O. Box 360009, Milpitas, CA 95036, United States of America

First Published in March 2012
Typeset in Bembo 11/13 [CP]

A catalogue record for this book is available from the British Library
Library of Congress cataloging in publication data

A Journey to God: Reflections on the Hikam of Ibn Ata'illah
Jasser Auda
p. cm.
Includes bibliographical references
ISBN 9781905837168
1. Islam – West 1. Title.
BP65.G7M37 2002
297.049109031- 97-41874 CIP

JASSER AUDA currently teaches Islamic Studies at the Qatar Faculty of Islamic Studies in Doha. He memorized the Quran and received traditional studies in Islamic sciences in Al-Azhar Mosque in Cairo. He was a founding director of the Maqasid Research Center in London. He wrote two PhD theses on the Philosophy of Islamic Law at the University of Wales, UK, and on Systems Analysis at the University of Waterloo, Canada. Dr Jasser Auda has published a number of books in Arabic and English, and translated several key books including Sheikh Mohammad al-Ghazali's *Muslim Women between Backward Traditions and Modern Innovations* (from Arabic to English), and the former Archbishop Rowan Williams's *Islam, Christianity and Pluralism* (from English to Arabic). He is the author of *Averröes's Premier of the Jurist: Synopsis and Commentary* (in Arabic) and *Maqasid al-Shari'ah as Philosophy of Islamic law: A System's Approach* (in English). Dr Jasser Auda is also a visiting lecturer to universities in Egypt, Canada, Qatar, and India.

CONTENTS

INTRODUCTION

The Start of the Journey

There is no real distance between you and Him in order for you to journey. And the connection between you and Him is not cut such that you must mend it.

IN THE NAME OF GOD, THE LORD OF MERCY, THE GIVER OF MERCY

ALL PRAISE IS DUE TO GOD. Peace and blessings be upon the Prophet Muhammad, his family, his Companions, and whoever follows his guidance until the Last Day. We ask God Almighty to bestow on us His Mercy and His Grace, out of His Mercy and Generosity, not because of what we do or we have ever done, and not because of what we know or we have ever known; only out of His pure Mercy and Generosity. God alone is All-Knowing and we do not know. God alone is All-Powerful, and we have no power.

And God alone is the One who makes certain things happen and prevents other things from happening. We seek refuge in Him and we rely on Him alone. We ask Him to protect us against our ignorance and false illusion, to mend our flaws, to keep us on the straight path, and to guide us to what pleases Him.

We ask Him to make this journey that we are starting here a journey towards some true change in ourselves. In fact, it is impossible to change one's self toward a better state, or to ascend in the levels of conciseness and awareness without God's bounty and help: *Verily, you cannot guide aright everyone whom you love: but it is God who guides him that wills to be guided; and He is fully aware of all who would let themselves be guided* (Quran 28:56).[1]

But God promised us that if we are grateful to Him, He will give us more, and if we ask Him to forgive our mistakes, He will shower upon us His forgiveness as well as His blessings, materially and spiritually. He also promised that if we pray wholeheartedly, He will answer our prayers, and if we rely on Him, we will definitely succeed. In short, everything that we dream to achieve in this journey depends upon how much we rely on Him, turn to Him, seek His help, and pray to Him. Whatever good comes our way will be His choice, and He always chooses the best of circumstances for those who rely on Him.

This book is meant to be a 'journey'—a journey for God, with God, and to God, although He is truly close to us, much closer than we ever think. *And if My servants ask you about Me—behold, I am near* (Quran 2:186). *We are closer to the human than his jugular* (Quran 50:16). In Ibn Ata's words: "There is no real distance between you and Him in order for you to journey. And the connection between you and Him is not cut such that you must mend it." God is very near—we are the ones who are far away! God is closer to us than our jugular veins—we are the ones who are disconnected! This is why we must "journey" to Him, and learn how to come closer to Him.

Throughout our journey, we will learn manners; manners with God, not with people. We will learn to improve our character so that we are fit to be God's servants. This is a very important side of Islam that we often forget and do not give due attention to.

Here, we are not referring to the rituals of Islam or the laws of Islam. We are concerned with the spirit and the feelings of the heart while we perform these rituals or apply these laws in our practical lives. Here, we will not learn about the rules of the lawful and forbidden, but rather about how to discover our faults, humble ourselves, and offer sincere repentance to God. We will not learn about the rules of performing ablution and prayer, but rather about how to concentrate in our prayers and be ready to receive the cleansing light of ablution. We will not learn about the 'correct' movements of the body, but rather about the correct state of the heart; how to rely on God, how to surrender to God, how to humble ourselves before God, how to remember God, how to be content with His decrees, and how to reflect on His incredible creation. When we learn all this, we will know how to smile from our hearts and how to be happier people! *To a happy state shall indeed attain he who causes this self to grow in purity, and truly lost is he who buries it in darkness* (Quran 91:9–10).

'Purification of the Soul' is one of the Islamic branches of knowledge (or sciences) which some people call Sufism, and others call the science of hearts, of inner souls, of humbleness, of manners, the divinely-bestowed science, or even spirituality. In our journey to God, however, we are not concerned with names, classifications, and terminologies. We only care about the meanings, the purposes, and the essences.

However, it is valid and rational to ask: why do we need a separate 'science' or branch of knowledge for the purification of hearts, spirituality, or what is popularly known as Sufism?

The answer is that any science, including the religious sciences, develops based on the need for it. In the early days of Islam, there were no sciences of *tafsir* (interpretation), of *fiqh* (Islamic law), of *hadith* (prophetic traditions), of *rijal* (hadith narrators), of *usul al-fiqh* (philosophy of Islamic law), of *dawa* (Islamic call), or *ilm al-kalam* (Islamic philosophy of religion). But as times changed and people found themselves in dire need of such disciplines, scholars developed and classified such sciences for those who seek knowledge, and for those who wish to transfer their knowledge to others. Sufism is no exception.

And if you want to learn the science of *tafsir* (interpretation), for example, you must find the right experts in this field and study with them. It is a branch of knowledge with a philosophy, principles, and well-known major works written by principal scholars in the field, as with other disciplines, be they in the field of religion, the social sciences, or humanities. Sufism is no exception.

And every seeker of a science goes through different stages; from the beginner's stage to the stage of researchers and experts. Like other branches of Islamic knowledge, Sufism, spirituality, or purification of the soul (regardless of the name it is given) takes the seeker through these stages.

Note that some Sufis deviated from Sufism itself and what it is about, and others took extreme positions that the overwhelming majority of Muslims disagree with. Again, these deviations are not unique to Sufism. Other scholars of other sciences have also abused their sciences in one way or another. But this certainly does not render the whole science, or branch of knowledge, irrelevant, immoral, or forbidden.

Thus, we should not abandon Sufism just because some Sufis deviated from its right course, or because some Sufis fail to understand some fundamental Islamic concepts or address some essential contemporary issues. Some Sufis, for example, misunderstand the concept of relying on God and distort this great Islamic concept into laziness and apathy. Other Sufis misunderstand the virtue of hope in God's Mercy and take it as a permission to sin, as if they were immune from heavenly punishment. Likewise, some Sufis misunderstand the concept of 'fear of God' and turn it into a state of hopelessness, and so on. But all these deviations should not distract us from the purpose and aims of Sufism. First and foremost, Sufism aims at purifying one's soul until it reaches a level of excellence (*ihsan*) in knowing God and worshipping Him.

Now, who is qualified to teach us such knowledge? The answer is well explained in our Islamic heritage. The scholars most qualified to teach the purification of the soul are those who have mastered both kinds of knowledge, that is, the knowledge of the apparent and the knowledge of the soul, which means the knowledge of *fiqh* (law; knowledge about the lawful and the forbidden) and the knowledge of *haqiqa* (Truth), respectively. We cannot learn about the Truth without keeping the law in mind and observing its rules and moral limits.

While many Muslims simply equate *fiqh* with *sharia* (the Islamic way of life), *fiqh* is, in fact, only one part of the *sharia*. The knowledge of the *sharia* is much broader, and indeed it includes Sufism. One's conduct with God and the purification of the soul are part and parcel of the Islamic way of life (*sharia*) revealed to Muhammad ﷺ.

In this book, we embark on a spiritual journey to our Lord. Our teacher is a scholar who mastered the knowledge of the apparent and the knowledge of the soul. He is Ibn Ata, Master, Imam, and Shaykh Abu al-Fadl Taj al-Din Ahmad b. Muhammad b. Abd al-Karim, Ibn Ata-Allah al-Sakandari (may God have mercy on him), a great authority in Islamic spirituality, Islamic law, hadith, Arabic language, and other branches of knowledge.

Ibn Ata's masterpiece and most famous contribution to knowledge was written in the form of *hikam* (words of wisdom), in which each *hikma* (maxim, or word of wisdom) discusses a specific topic and guides believers one step along the Path. In my view, the words of wisdom (*hikam*) are meant to be a step-by-step spiritual journey to God, in the true sense of the word, from its start to its end, along the steps that Ibn Ata mastered and prescribed. This book is a selection of thirty of these *hikam*, presented in the form of "steps" along one's journey to/with God.

The journey begins with repentance to God, cherishing hope in His Mercy, learning sincerity to Him, relying on Him, reflecting upon His creation, and searching deep into one's soul for one's flaws. The journey ends by reaching a level of awareness, humbleness, satisfaction, and excellence in order "to worship God as though you are seeing Him, and while you see Him not yet truly He sees you," as the Prophet Muhammad ﷺ said.

Ibn Ata-Allah (whose name means, literally, the son of God's gift) was indeed gifted with wisdom and knowledge; *God grants wisdom unto whom He wills: and whoever is granted wisdom has indeed been granted wealth abundant* (Quran 2:269). Ibn Ata was born in 647 AH/1250 ACE. He grew up, lived, and died (709 AH/1309 ACE) in Alexandria, Egypt, may God bless his soul. Ibn Ata left behind a large number of students that he taught and a fine collection of books that he wrote. His teachers, students, and contemporaries acknowledged his qualifications to issue fatwas in matters of faith according to the rules of Sufism, and in matters of practical life according to the rules of Maliki *fiqh*.

Each chapter begins with a translation/interpretation of Ibn Ata's eloquent and concise words. My humble comments start with some questions about the meaning of the *hikma* at hand. Then, I offer answers to those questions by explaining Ibn Ata's words in a way that is less concise and somewhat simpler than the high language he used. I attempt to support every new concept with evidence from the Quran and the Sunna (Prophet Muhammad's tradition). My objective from this citation of original Islamic texts is to explain the originality and 'authenticity' of the Sufi terminology and expressions that Ibn Ata proposed. Sometimes, along the Sufi journey, we come across expressions that are, unfortunately, unfamiliar to most Muslims, such as those that refer to the "virtue of isolation," "not relying on one's good deeds," "not feeling content with oneself," or the importance of *baraka* (heavenly blessing). As I show here, Sufi expressions do, in fact, have their roots in the Quranic and prophetic language.

For example, the idea of 'isolation' is confirmed with reference to the Prophet Muhammad's *itikaf* (isolation for worship) in the mountains and in the mosque during the month of Ramadan and other months as well. The idea of 'not relying on one's good deeds' is supported by the hadith in which the Prophet ﷺ says: "None amongst you can enter Paradise because of his good deeds alone . . . except with God's Mercy."[2] The idea of dissatisfaction with oneself is supported by the verse which reads, *But nay! I call to witness the accusing voice of man's own conscience!* (Quran 75:2). Likewise, the concept of *baraka*, or blessing, is mentioned and explained in a number Quranic verses and prophetic traditions.

I also try to elaborate on the relationship between these words of wisdom and the universal laws of God (*al-sunan al-ilahiyya*). These are the higher, consistent, and fundamental laws that God made to govern everything in our universe, such as the balance of unity, parity, and diversity in our creation and in the creation of everything, and the cyclical changes in human development and in the development of every society, trend, and phenomena. Universal laws also include other principles that govern human life in its individual and societal forms, including justice, trials, repayment, and other principles that are explained throughout the book.

The original form of this book was thirty short speeches which I delivered in Arabic during *tarawih* (night) prayers throughout the month of Ramadan 1429 AH/2008 ACE, at the Hira Mosque in Muqattam in Cairo, Egypt. This beautiful mosque was built by the late Shaykh Abdallah Shehata of Dar al-Ulum Faculty of Cairo University, and is now faithfully maintained by his wonderful family. The lessons were originally divided over the thirty days of the month of Ramadan, and then published in a book in Arabic (*al-Suluk ma'a-Allah* [Cairo: Dar al-Hidaya, 2010]) in the form of twenty-eight chapters, in addition to an introduction and a conclusion. The present English work is a different book, though it is based on the ideas, themes, and the division of chapters of the Arabic book.[3]

The *Hikam* [Words of wisdom] has been commented on and explained in different forms by both classic and contemporary scholars. Of the classic commentaries, the ones made by Imams Ibn Abbad, Ahmad Zarruq, and Ibn Ajiba were the best that I came across. I also benefited greatly from the commentaries of contemporary scholars, especially our late Shaykh Muhammad al-Ghazali, Shaykh Said Hawwa, and Shaykh Ali Jumaa.

I do not consider this humble book to be a new commentary; it is, rather, a compilation of some personal reflections on Ibn Ata's wisdom, which I pray God benefits me with and benefits others too. It is impossible to know how God will benefit others with a word you say or a book you write. All I have is hope in Him, and I know from experience that the Generous Almighty takes people who have hope in Him a long way!

As the next words of wisdom will explain, our flaws, shortcomings, and mistakes should not stop us from working, hoping, and also expecting God's infinite Grace, Mercy, and Bounty. Let us seek God's assistance and send peace and blessings upon the prophets, their wise followers, and those who followed their path to God.

JASSER AUDA

Doha, Rabi al-Thani 1432/March 2011

FIRST STEP

Repentance and hope

If you find yourself having less hope in God when you make a mistake, then realise that you are only relying on your work, not on God's Mercy.

IN THE NAME OF GOD, THE LORD OF MERCY, THE GIVER OF MERCY

WHEN I HAVE an intention to start or re-start a spiritual journey to God, I have to ask myself: where should I start? And what should I take with me on this journey? Should I recall the good deeds I have done and take them as my provisions in this journey? The answer given by Ibn Ata in these words of wisdom is: No! Do not rely even on your good deeds, rather start your journey to God by simply turning your heart to Him, putting your trust in Him alone, and hoping only for His Mercy and Bounty to carry you through your journey.

However, one might ask: Is not receiving God's mercy a result of good deeds? And, does God's mercy and bounty stop when I have no good deeds? The answer is no. *Now if God were to take humans immediately to task for all the evil that they do, He would not leave a single living creature upon the face of earth* (Quran 16:61). Therefore, it is not a matter of 'deserving' or 'earning' God's mercy and bounties. It is a matter of relying on God's mercy and bounties to receive them despite one's shortcomings. This is the right start for the right course.

But turning to God and hoping for His mercy must be accompanied by repentance from one's mistakes and errors. According to God's universal laws, in order to put something in a certain place, there must be room and space for this addition. Faith and light is no exception. Thus, if we want to fill our hearts with faith, light, and God's remembrance, we should first find room in our hearts that is not occupied with other sorts of objects and desires. Only then can we fill our hearts with goodness, or, according to the Sufi expression: Purity, then beauty, then light (*al-takhalli thum al-tahalli thum al-tajalli*).

Therefore, we must start this journey by repenting to God of our shortcomings. *And always, O you believers—all of you—turn unto God in repentance, so that you might attain to a happy state!* (Quran 24:31).

Repentance should be accompanied by a certain feeling, as Ibn Ata emphasises here in these words of wisdom—hope in God. But why is hope necessary for repentance? And how does this relate to one's journey? This is what Ibn Ata explains here. He says: "If you find yourself having less hope in God when you make a mistake, then realise that you are only relying on your work, not on God's Mercy." This means that if you are keen to rely on God's mercy and put all your trust in Him, make sure that you are not self-righteous! Do not think that you have achieved virtue because of your efforts and deeds. And among the signs of one's relying on his deeds, more than on God's mercy and bounty, is the decrease in hope when one makes a mistake. Hope in Him should always be at the same level.

Scholars count four necessary conditions for a correct repentance. First, one should feel remorse for the mistake he made. Second, one should stop making the mistake, if it is a continuing habit. Third, one should have a sincere determination not to repeat the same mistake in the future. Fourth, if the mistake relates to people's rights, one must return to people what one owes them. A sincere repentant must meet these four conditions.

The first condition is feeling remorse for the mistake. The Prophet Muhammad ﷺ said: "Remorse is repentance."[4] The second condition is to refrain from committing the mistake itself; a hypocrite is one who continues the mistake while claiming repentance from it. The third condition is to have a sincere determination never to repeat the same mistake in the future. One cannot feel regret about a mistake and give it up, while also having an intention to commit the mistake again in the near or distant future.

But if it happens that—God forbid—one falls into the same error again, the only solution is to repeat the same process again, that is, renew the repentance, renew the remorse and regret, and decide not to fall again. And so on. One must know that God is Most Forgiving and Most Merciful. God does not mind accepting one's (sincere) repentance again and again. On the contrary, God is pleased when His servant repents to Him, as the Prophet said.

As for the fourth condition, scholars say that if the mistake one has committed relates to people's rights, one must make amends. For example, if one unlawfully takes something, it must be returned. If an injustice is committed, it must be corrected. Scholars also mention that one must seek people's pardon if one speaks ill of them. And so on.

Ibn Ata assumes the fulfilment of these conditions, and adds that one must have a feeling of hope in the Lord. This is not a "condition" but rather an ethic (with God). *These it is who may hope for God's grace: for God is Much-Forgiving, a Dispenser of Grace* (Quran 2:218).

Sometimes, hope is lost, and one asks himself: How should I look forward to God's grace after making all these mistakes? How will God accept my repentance? This questioning itself is a mistake! A feeling that your mistakes are too great and too many for God to forgive goes against the very belief in God, the Merciful. This will cause one to lose hope in God's mercy and eventually lead to despair and hopelessness. *And who—other than those who have utterly lost their way—could ever abandon the hope of their Sustainer's grace?* (Quran 15:56).

One who loses hope is not really relying on God. Rather, one is relying on his weak self, limited mind, and humble actions. Of course, this does not mean that he should stop working and say that he has hope. This is also wrong. Relying on God is a feeling in the heart while the body is in action.

Here, Ibn Ata says that, regardless of how grave one's mistakes, they should not affect one's hope in God's mercy. If one repents sincerely to God, God surely will accept his repentance. The Prophet is reported to have said: "A person who has repented of a sin sincerely is exactly like the person who has never sinned at all."[5] And he said: "God says: O son of Adam, as long as you call upon Me and ask of

Me, I shall forgive you for what you have done, and I shall not mind! O son of Adam, were you to come to Me with sins nearly as great as the earth, I would forgive you, and I shall not mind."[6]

Hope should not be affected by the gravity of one's mistakes. Rather, one should make a sincere intention to repent to God and simply expect His mercy. The Prophet also said: "God says: I am as My servant expects Me to be! So, let him think of Me as he wishes."[7]

Here Ibn Ata says, if you find yourself having less hope in God when you make a mistake, then realise that you are only relying on your work, not on God's mercy. And this meaning is similar to the meaning of the hadith in which the Prophet ﷺ says: "None amongst you can enter Paradise because of his deeds alone." The Companions asked: "God's Messenger, not even you?" The Prophet said: "Not even myself, unless God bestows His forgiveness and mercy on me."[8]

In this hadith, the Prophet ﷺ says: "There is none whose deeds alone would entitle him to enter Paradise." Does this mean that we lose hope in God's mercy? Of course not. What is meant is that we must not to rely on our deeds, but place our trust in God's mercy. This is the same message that Ibn Ata conveyed in his words of wisdom.

But so much hope should not turn into a feeling of immunity, that is, to feel immune and saved from God's punishment, regardless of what you do. *And they say, "The fire will most certainly not touch us for more than a limited number of days"* (Quran 2:80). This verse was revealed regarding some of the previous nations, those who believed that they are God's chosen people, regardless of their actions and regardless of what they do in this life. Nowadays, some Muslims think that as long as they are Muslims, they can do whatever they want and they will not be harmed. God says: *But none feels secure from God's deep devising save people who are lost* (Quran 7:99).

Hope should not become a false state of immunity or a guarantee that God will bestow His mercy regardless of what one does. The only guarantee is one's actual admission to Paradise. Abu Bakr al-Siddiq (may God be pleased with him) said: "I would not feel safe from God's deep devising even if one of my feet was in Paradise and the other is still outside."

Thus, we should strike a balance between hope and awe. Balance is a universal law that we must struggle to find in everything. Balance in repentance is to repent sincerely to God, not only out of hope in His mercy but also out of fear of His repayment.

Some disbelievers have an illusion of hopelessness. They might want to turn to their Lord, but they think that He will never forgive the evil they did. Therefore, they continue in their wrong ways. God says: *Your Sustainer has willed upon Himself the law of grace and mercy—so that if any of you does an evil deed out of ignorance, and thereafter repents and lives righteously, God shall be Much-Forgiving, a Dispenser of Grace. And thus clearly do We spell out Our messages so that the path of those who are lost in sin might be distinct [from that of the righteous who repent]* (Quran 6:54–55). The sinner is the one who rejects this divine offer of repentance. Here we must strike a balance between hope and awe.

Thus, the first step on this path is to affirm your hope in God's mercy and simply turn your heart to Him. This is the first stop in the long, or short journey.

SECOND STEP

The dominance of the universal laws of God

A human will, however strong it is, can never pierce through the veils of destiny.

IN THE NAME OF GOD, THE LORD OF MERCY, THE GIVER OF MERCY

We began our spiritual journey to God with words of wisdom that guide us to have infinite hope in God's mercy; we should never doubt our hope in God because of past mistakes. God is Merciful and forgives any mistake as long as there is sincere repentance.

Sometimes, when one begins a new journey or a new resolution, one is full of energy, aspiration, and enthusiasm. Thus, he tries to change himself, his family, society, country, and the whole world overnight! People sometimes forget what Ibn Ata called "the veils of destiny." Ibn Ata says, "A human will, however strong it is, can never pierce through the veils of destiny." What does this mean?

It means that despite our strong will and determination to do something, we cannot pierce through God's destinies. These destines are universal laws (*sunan*) that are consistent and prevailing. God says: *No change will you ever find in God's laws (sunna); yea, no deviation will you ever find in God's laws!* (Quran 35:44). This is how the universe is created naturally. *Behold, everything have We created in due measure* (Quran 54:49).

Among these universal laws is God's creation of life according to certain conditions that lead to certain results. No human being, Muslim or non-Muslim, can ever pierce through the veils of destiny and achieve specific outcomes without following the right means, reasons, steps, circumstances, and laws (*sunan*).

For instance, God says: *Do humans think that on their saying, "We have attained faith," they will be left to themselves, and will not be put to a test?* (Quran 29:2). This is the law of trials, or testing people with hardship in this life. If anyone claims that they believe in God and have attained faith, God will test them with some of this world's trials. No one can avoid this test however strong their will or determination. This is a universal law.

Another example is the universal laws of change. One of these laws is the need for any process of change to progress in due time and graduation. Time has been created by God for people such that everyone recognises its nature and importance according to his own knowledge. Only God is not bound by time. Time simply does not apply to God. It is only a human reality, and God decreed that goals should take time to be achieved. We cannot change the world or even change ourselves in a moment. This will never happen. You may try to learn the Quran by heart as fast as you can. But you should not memorise the Quran in a week or a month. And if you commit it to memory in a month, you will forget it all in a month or even less. We must let things take their necessary time and surrender to God's laws and destiny. In fact, people who try to make abrupt changes in themselves or the world around them often fail and most likely despair!

Muslim jurists state the following maxim: "A person who hastens something before its due time will be punished by being deprived of it." In other words, if one ignores the fact that time is needed for any significant change in this world, one not only delays the desired change, but will most likely lose it forever.

Among the veils of destiny that every Muslim must also note is what scholars call the "duty of the time" (*wajib al-waqt*). Throughout one's life, there are different stages that carry with them different duties and responsibilities. For example, at one stage, you must work hard to earn money to get married. This might take much time and effort for a while. At another stage, you might have to look after young children or elderly parents, and take care of their affairs. At a later stage of life, when children are older and more independent, you may have financial security, but will have to work hard to achieve a certain higher goal, or fulfil your duties in a public service office, for example. At a different stage, the duty of the time might involve travel in pursuit of knowledge, or perhaps, God forbid, taking a long break for health reasons. In all of the above cases you cannot pierce through the veils of destiny. When you are sick, you cannot behave as you did when you were healthy, and when you are seventy, you cannot behave as you did when you were forty!

This is an important step on the path to God: always pay attention to the duty of your time, as much as you understand it. Believe in God's wisdom in everything He gives or takes away, and surrender to the laws of the universe and the veils of destiny.

It is also important on the path to God, after completing a duty or turning a new page, to turn to the Lord in worship and devotion. The Prophet ﷺ was addressed in the Quran by the following: *Hence, when you are freed [from hardship], remain steadfast, and turn all your attention to your Lord in devotion and love* (Quran 94:7–8).

And even when we turn to God in devotion, we must still do this step by step. The Prophet is reported to have said "Surely this religion is firm, so walk through it step by step."[9] This means that even embracing religion in one's daily life should be undertaken gradually. You cannot learn all the ideals and rules or practice them in one day. The Prophet continued, saying "This is because the traveller who is too harsh on his riding animal will not reach his destination, and the riding animal will die." However strong your determination and aspiration is, your body is like that riding animal, and you need to apply the same law to it.

The previous words of wisdom taught us to strike a balance between awe and hope, and these words of wisdom also teach us to strike a balance between our will and divine destiny, or between the steps we aspire to advance by on God's path, and the "veils of destiny," as the Shaykh put it. These two rules of balance will allow us to advance to the next step on our journey.

THIRD STEP

Relying on God

Save yourself from worrying. Someone else already took care of your affairs for you.

IN THE NAME OF GOD, THE LORD OF MERCY, THE GIVER OF MERCY

Relying on God (*tawakkul*) is an important Islamic concept that is mentioned many times in the Quran, but often misunderstood in the popular Sufi conception. It is a misunderstanding that leads to deviation from the true religion of God, and can cause failure in both religious and worldly affairs. This happens when relying on God (*tawakkul*) is mixed with apathy (*tawaakul*). In the name of relying on God, many people who claimed to be Sufis—during some dark periods of history—chose a lifestyle of laziness, begging, and uselessness (traditionally called *bitala* in Arabic). The spread of this idea amongst the religious people left Muslims' public affairs to be run by the least qualified and the least pious.

So, how do we practice reliance on God (*tawakkul*) properly? Ibn Ata advises: "Save yourself from worrying (*tadbir*). Someone else already took care of your affairs for you." What is meant by *tadbir* here?

Tadbir in Arabic means considering the results of actions. Thus, *tadbir* is closely connected with outcomes. Ibn Ata says that it is with regard to outcomes that we should practice reliance on God and trust in Him. God says: *Then, when you have decided upon a course of action, place your trust in God: for, verily, God loves those who place their trust in Him* (Quran 3:159); *In God, then, let the believers place their trust!* (Quran

3:160), *they answered, "God is enough for us; and how excellent a guardian is He!"* (Quran 3:173).

Concerning oneself with working on the means is desirable, but worrying is being concerned about the ends and outcomes, which are up to God in any case! A believer strives to achieve goals and relies on God. It is God who is in control of everything. *And who is it that is in control of all that exists?* (Quran 10:31). One must remind himself of this clear question raised in the Quran.

And if God is in charge, then we have to follow the means and leave the outcomes to Him. The Prophet ﷺ gave us a perfect example to teach us the meaning of relying on God. He said: "If you had all relied on God as you should rely on Him, then He would have provided for you as He provides for the birds, who wake up hungry in the morning and return with full stomachs at dusk."

We are like these birds. And the birds never stand on one branch of a tree waiting for grain to come! They move continuously from one branch to another until they find the grain. The bird's work is to do its best to find the grain; but providing the bird with the grain is God's work.

Therefore, a believer should follow the means and leave the outcomes to God. Some people, however, do not follow any means. They stay in the mosque all the time, and beg people for their food and clothes. They argue that *tadbir* is not their job. This situation did happen at the time of the Prophet ﷺ. It is reported that a man used to stay at the mosque all the time, arguing that he was devoting himself to worship God. The Prophet asked about who supports him. The Prophet was told that the man's brother supports him. The Prophet commented: "His brother is better than him." Umar b. al-Khattab advised some people, who lived at the mosque and claimed to be "relying on God," by his famous words: "The sky does not rain gold or silver."

Relying on God is also desirable when success is not attained even after following every necessary means. In this case, one might say: "O God, I have done my best, what should I do? I can only put my trust in You." One must understand that sometimes God withholds success or takes away the means from people so they return to Him and rely on Him. This is a valuable God-given gift.

Finally, relying on God is not inconsistent with many activities today—planning, carrying out feasibility studies, analysing the market, and so forth. All of this is part of relying on God because, by planning, organising, and studying, we are following the means of success. If you have a commercial project, for example, you have to make a feasibility study of the market, and rely on God. Then, if you lose, it is God's decree, and if you win, it is also God's decree. In both cases, you do not have to worry about the outcomes now.

Even in religious issues, like calling people to belief or seeking excellence in worship, we can only do our best and leave the rest to God. He says: *It is not for you [O Prophet] to make people follow the right path, since it is God alone who guides whom He wills* (Quran 2:272), and *Verily, you cannot guide aright everyone whom you love: but it is God who guides those who are willing to be guided; and He is fully aware of the truly guided ones* (Quran 28:56).

Ibn Ata says: "Save yourself from worrying. Someone else already took care of your affairs for you." By "someone else," he meant the Almighty One who provides the means and decides the outcomes.

FOURTH STEP

Sincerity to God

Actions are like statues that only come to life with the spirit of sincerity.

IN THE NAME OF GOD, THE LORD OF MERCY, THE GIVER OF MERCY

Sincerity to God is more fundamental than reliance on God, since it has to do with a deeper level of faith in Him. Yet, it was important to affirm our reliance on God and hope in His mercy before discussing sincerity. This is because pure sincerity to God is subtle and difficult to achieve without first having hope in God's grace and strong reliance on Him.

"Sincerity is one of God's 'secrets' that He plants in the heart of whomsoever He loves," the Prophet Muhammad said. And sincerity to God is essential for our journey. In Ibn Ata's words: "Actions are like statues that only come to life with the spirit of sincerity." If we imagine a simile between an action and a human body, then the action devoid of sincerity is like a body without a soul; a dead body.

What is sincerity? It means that your intention (Arabic: *niyya*, *maqsid*) is honest and true to God. The Prophet ﷺ said: "Actions are according to intentions and every man shall have that which he intended. Thus, he whose migration is for God and His messenger, his migration is for God and His messenger, and he whose migration is to achieve some worldly benefit or to take a woman in marriage, his migration is for that for which he migrated."[10]

The hadith talks about two examples of migration (both with the Prophet, from Mecca to Medina). Some people migrated only to do business or to get married; they will be rewarded only for their intentions. However, the Companions who migrated purely for the sake of God and to support His messenger, their reward is also according to their intention. In fact, God told us specifically their reward in the Quran: *And as for the first and foremost of those who have migrated [to Medina] and of those who have supported them, as well as those who follow them in [the way of] righteousness—God is well-pleased with them, and well-pleased are they with Him. And for them has He readied gardens through which running waters flow, therein to abide beyond the count of time: this is the triumph supreme!* (Quran 9:100).

Having a pure intention is very important: without this intention, worship becomes a show, with the intention to please people, not to please God. Worship with an intention to please people is an act of polytheism and hypocrisy, God forbid. In fact, God describes the hypocrites in the Quran as follows: *Behold, the hypocrites seek to deceive God—while it is He who causes them to be deceived by themselves. And when they rise to pray, they rise reluctantly, only to be seen and praised by people, remembering God but seldom* (Quran 4:142). And amongst those who deserve blame and punishment in the hereafter, God mentions *those who want only to be seen and praised* (Quran 107:6–7).

Every action should be done with a pure intention to please God Almighty. We must ask ourselves, why are we doing this, giving this charity, going on *hajj* (pilgrimage), helping this person, offering this prayer, reading this book? And so on.

And by sincerity, we can turn our daily habits into rewarded acts of worship. Eating, drinking, going to work, getting married, travelling, buying, selling, and all other actions and habits can be acts of worship for which we will be rewarded.

For example, one may eat in order not to feel hungry. But one can also eat and have a sincere intention to be able to worship God. This intention makes eating itself a rewarded act of worship. One may dress well in order to look good. But one can also have the additional intention to thank God, show modesty, please others, and so on. We may work only for the salary, but we can also work to give charity, to perform *hajj*, to support our families, and so on.

All of these are intentions that turn our habits into acts of worship, if they are sincere and true, and give us momentum in our spiritual journey to God. Some people journey to God only through regular prayers at their fixed times, through *zakah* (charity) when it is due, and through other specified acts of worship. They could, however, journey much faster if they learn how to transform daily habits into additional acts of worship.

One of the Sufi imams heard someone knocking on his door while he was with some students. Before opening the door, the imam mentioned to his students several sincere intentions that he recalled: if he opens the door and finds a poor man, he will give him charity; if he finds a person who needs help, he will help him; if he finds a lost person, he will show him the way; if he finds a little child, he will be kind to him; if he finds an old man, he will show him respect; if he finds a student of knowledge, he will teach him, and so on. The simplest act of opening that door became—by the man's pure intention—a number of acts of worship!

Ibn Ata says: "Actions are like statues that only come to life with the spirit of sincerity." Let us always ask God to grant us sincerity, to help us turn our habits into sincere acts of worship, and devote our lives to Him alone. *Say: "Behold, my prayer, and my acts of worship, and my living and my dying are for God alone, the Lord of all the worlds. In whose divinity none has a share: for thus have I been bidden—and I shall always be foremost among those who surrender themselves unto Him"* (Quran 6:162, 163).

FIFTH STEP

Reflection

Bury yourself in the land of anonymity. A seed that is never buried underground will never produce. There is nothing more beneficial to the heart than isolation that allows it to enter a state of reflection.

IN THE NAME OF GOD, THE LORD OF MERCY, THE GIVER OF MERCY

The next step in our journey is to develop a deeper understanding and a stronger heart, to feel all the meanings we have discussed so far: repentance, awe, hope, reliance on God, and sincerity. The way we can achieve this is, as Ibn Ata suggests, through reflection.

Reflection is a marvellous form of worship that advances us on our path to God and helps us realise our spirituality. The Prophet ﷺ said: "Reflection for one hour is better than praying for sixty years." Even though this hadith is "weak" in terms of authenticity, its meaning is correct. This is because a person who takes the time to reflect on God and/or His creation for one hour is actually worshipping God through deep knowledge, with sincere feeling, and spiritual light.

Verily, in the creation of the heavens and the earth, and in the succession of night and day, there are indeed messages for those who are endowed with insight. They are the ones who remember God when they stand, and when they sit, and when they lie down to sleep, and thus reflect on the creation of the heavens and the earth: O our Sustainer! You have not created this without meaning and purpose. Limitless are You in Your glory! (Quran 3:190–191).

Those who are endowed with insight reflect on the creation of the heavens and earth and the alternation of day and night. Many people possess abundant information about the universe in their minds, but lack feeling in their hearts. But those who truly reflect on the universe keep in their minds the Creator of the universe. They think about the heavens and the earth in terms of the Greatness of the Maker of the heavens and the earth. This reflection eventually leads people to say: "You have not created this without meaning and purpose."

Reflection also creates a feeling of awe of God. *Are you not aware that God sends down water from the skies, whereby We bring forth fruits of many hues—just as in the mountains there are streaks of white and red of various shades, as well as others raven-black—and as there are in men, and in crawling beasts, and in cattle, too, many hues? Only people of knowledge stand truly in awe of God: for they alone comprehend that* (Quran 35:28).

In these words of wisdom, Ibn Ata points out something that helps in the process of reflection—this is to maintain anonymity and isolation. Anonymity and isolation are also Sufi concepts that many people misunderstand and practice in a way that goes against the true objectives and spirit of Islam.

The Arabic word used for anonymity here is *khumul*, which could also mean laziness. Ibn Ata is referring to a state of obscurity from fame. This state is achieved when one isolates himself from people for a limited period, not indefinitely! Monastic isolation, in the sense of separating oneself from the world out of dedication to God, is against the teachings of Islam. The Prophet Muhammad made it clear that, "there is no monasticism in Islam," and he said: "A believer who interacts with people and is patient when they harm him is better than a Muslim who does not mingle with people and does not have to be patient when they harm him."[11] Thus, a normal believer interacts with people, works, marries, visits relatives and neighbours, enjoins good and forbids evil, befriends people, and so on. However, occasionally, he keeps himself in a temporary isolation, for the sake of reflection.

Is Ibn Ata's call for "isolation" Islamic? Is there evidence in the prophetic tradition to support it? Or is it an innovation in the true faith?

There are clear lessons and evidences of isolation, in addition to the Prophet's periods of worship in the cave of Hira before and after the revelation, in the Prophet's retreat in the mosque (*itikaf*) to worship God during the month of Ramadan and during other months.

The Companions (may God be pleased with them) reported that the Prophet used to perform *itikaf* every year in the month of Ramadan for ten days, and in the year of his death, he stayed in the mosque in Ramadan for twenty days.

Aisha (may God be pleased with her) reported that the Prophet used to perform *itikaf* in the last ten days of Ramadan until he died, then his wives continued to do *itikaf* after he died. She also reported that the Prophet once performed *itikaf* for twenty days during the month of Shawwal.

Ibn Ata makes a connection here between this prophetic tradition of *itikaf* and a divine universal law of creation. Every living creature; plants, animals, birds, or even humans, goes through a period in which it is isolated in darkness, before it starts to grow and produce. Seeds in the ground and embryos in eggs or wombs must grow, initially, in isolation, away from external factors.

A seed planted in the darkness of the earth goes through a period of nurturing and watering until it finally starts to form roots and a stem. Only then is it time for the plant to break through the soil and come out to the surface. Likewise, a foetus grows in the darkness of the mother's womb until its bones, organs, and nerves are formed, then it comes to life when it is ready to live in the outside environment.

Similarly, a heart/mind needs a retreat in a mosque or a place that is isolated from people, to reach a state of enlightenment. When the heart reaches this state, it can travel from the universe to its Maker, from the creatures to their Creator, and from the realm of signs, rules and rituals to the world of meanings, wisdom, and higher purposes. This temporary isolation takes the heart back to the purity of faith and a true connection with God! Otherwise, faith remains like a seed that was never buried underground, and will never produce, as Ibn Ata puts it. This is a universal law that no one can change or ignore.

Isolation for the sake of reflection has a number of other benefits. One benefit is that it helps in avoiding sins, such a gossip and backbiting. Another benefit is that it trains the servant to guard his tongue against its destructive vices. *A human is, above all else, always given to argument* (Quran 18:54). Isolation is also training to clear one's intentions from considering people and what they say. Though showing off may find its way to one's heart, even when alone. Ibn Ata says elsewhere: "Perhaps showing off has entered upon you, even when people do not see you." This is the case when one occupies himself with how people think about him, even when alone.

Sometimes we forget the work of the heart and focus on the work of the organs. This hardens the heart and leads to forgetfulness, and puts obstacles and difficulties in the course of one's journey to God. However, a reflective retreat, which the Shaykh advises us about here, makes the heart shine. "There is nothing more beneficial to the heart than isolation that allows it to enter a state of reflection."

SIXTH STEP

Clearing before shining

How can the mirror of the heart shine if material images cover it?
How can the heart journey to God if it is chained by its desires?
How can the heart ever hope to enter the divine presence
if it has not purified itself from its forgetfulness?

IN THE NAME OF GOD, THE LORD OF MERCY, THE GIVER OF MERCY

Reflection causes the light of faith to shine in the heart of the believer. However, the heart is like a mirror, Ibn Ata explains, and it has to be "pure" before it shines. He says: "There is nothing more beneficial to the heart than isolation that allows it to enter a state of reflection. How can the mirror of the heart shine if material images cover it? How can the heart journey to God if it is chained by its desires? How can the heart ever hope to enter the divine presence if it has not purified itself from its forgetfulness?" In other words, before beautifying the heart with the light of virtues, it must be purified from certain flaws. Here Ibn Ata mentions three such flaws: material images, desires, and forgetfulness.

Ibn Ata asks, how can the mirror of the heart shine if material images cover it? Sufis have an expression for anything other than God, which is *al-aghyar* (Arabic: the others). When the "others," such as material things, earthly objects, or even people, are imprinted on the heart, they act like pictures that are imprinted on a mirror. This is a wonderful simile that illustrates that it is impossible for a heart full of "others" to shine with light while it is in that state.

Certainly, this does not mean that we should ignore the material world, family, wealth, career, and so on. The question is, what is in the depth of the heart that receives the most attention and the most concern? Is it a pure heart that shines with light? *God is the Light of the heavens and the earth. The parable of His light is, as it were, that of a niche containing a lamp; the lamp is in glass, the glass shining like a radiant star: lit from a blessed tree—an olive tree that is neither of the east nor of the west, the oil whereof is so bright that it would well-nigh give light even though fire had not touched it: light upon light! God guides unto His light him whom He wills to be guided; and God propounds parables unto men, since God has full knowledge of all things. In the houses of worship which God has allowed to be raised...* (Quran 24:35–6). Therefore, it is in God's house and places of worship that isolation and reflection can produce the divine Light in the believer's heart. And light, by nature, will eliminate darkness.

The second flaw is what Ibn Ata called "desires." Ibn Ata asks, "How can the heart journey to God if it is chained by its desires?" Again, this does not mean that every desire is evil! Islam is not against desires and, in fact, did not prohibit them; Islam only regulates desires. God did not create desires in us, and then prohibit our expressing them completely. It is a universal law that instincts and natural human desires cannot be totally suppressed. In contrast to other belief systems, Islam does not prohibit natural desires or consider their denial a virtue. What is prohibited is the expression of specific desires under certain circumstances.

Thus, God did not prohibit anything that He made a characteristic of our nature, such as eating, quenching our thirst, sex, speaking, laughing, singing, and listening to music, and so on. However, Islam regulates these activities in a way that is moral, that is, eating should not be excessive, drinking alcohol is forbidden, speaking should be truthful and should not cause harm, sex should be within marriage, and so on.

But when it comes to isolation, meditation and reflection should not be mixed with desire, even lawful ones. God says: *do not lie with them skin to skin when you are abiding in meditation in houses of worship. These are the bounds set by God: do not, then, offend against them* (Quran 2:187). This is one of the rulings of *itikaf* (retreat in a mosque), and this verse is also evidence in Islamic law for the legality of *itikaf*. As for how the Prophet ﷺ applied this tradition (*sunna*), it is reported that he used to do *itikaf* in the last ten days of Ramadan. In the year in which he died, he retreated for twenty days. It is reported that he performed *itikaf* in months other than Ramadan. Therefore, *itikaf* is not only confined to Ramadan and it can be observed in other months, as part of the prophetic tradition.

In general, from the Islamic viewpoint the light of the heart does not contradict with desire. They only contradict each other when desire distracts or covers the heart so that it cannot journey to God. God says: *And God wants to turn unto you in His mercy, whereas those who follow only their own lusts want you to drift far away from the right path* (Quran 4:27).

The third flaw that Ibn Ata points to is forgetfulness. Ibn Ata asks, "How can the heart ever hope to enter the divine presence if it has not purified itself from its forgetfulness?" God's presence is what is expressed in the Quran in terms of God being "with" people, even though He is never absent, Glory be to Him. God says: *Behold, God is with those who believe!* (Quran 8:19), *seeing that God is with you, you are bound to rise high in the end; and never will He let your good deeds go to waste* (Quran 47:35), *and know that God is with those who are conscious of Him* (Quran 9:36), *and be patient in adversity: for, verily, God is with those who are patient in adversity* (Quran 8:46), *for, verily, God is with those who are conscious of Him and are doers of good withal!* (Quran 16:128). All those people; believers, doers of good deeds, those who are conscious of Him, the patient ones—they are all with God and in God's presence.

The question, then, is what prevents people from feeling or attaining God's presence? Ibn Ata says that forgetfulness and neglect of the remembrance of God is something we need to seek God's forgiveness from. Remembrance of God is what purifies the heart.

Every Muslim should devote part of his time to the remembrance of God. Do not say that you do not have time to remember God! This is unacceptable, because you can remember God in any circumstance and condition. And in terms of remembering Him in isolation, this is a matter of half an hour or an hour that can benefit the heart and make a difference. Therefore, Ibn Ata says in the next words of wisdom: "Postponing good deeds until you have free time is an indication of an immature soul."

We ask the Light of heavens and earth—as the Prophet asked Him—to grant us light "above us, below us, ahead of us, to the right, to the left, and in our hearts, and to make us sources of light."

SEVENTH STEP

Seizing time

Postponing good deeds until you have free time is an indication of an immature soul.

IN THE NAME OF GOD, THE LORD OF MERCY, THE GIVER OF MERCY

Sometimes we postpone the good that we have the intention to do and say: I will do that tomorrow, next week, next month, or next Ramadan. I will do that when I get married, when I get a promotion, when the children grow older, or when the weather gets better! Ibn Ata describes this attitude as an indication of an "immature soul."

In fact, doing good deeds is not a matter of having time. It is a matter of priorities. One leaves home every morning for a specific number of hours, and achieves a certain number of tasks every day. People normally do what is most important first, then what is less important, and so on. *God does not burden any human being with more than they have the ability to do* (Quran 2:286).

In Islamic law, if you have five minutes before the end of the allowed prayer period, and you have a number of things to do including your prayers, then it is an obligation to perform your prayers first. However, if there is serious harm that will happen because of you tending to your prayers (for example, a young child who will fall down the stairs or a blind person who needs help crossing the street), the obligation becomes to avoid that harm first, and then perform the prayer. In Islamic law this is called *fiqh al-awlawiyyat*, or the knowledge of priorities. We will address this topic in detail later, God willing.

The consideration of priorities, however, should not be an excuse to always postpone good work in the way of God. Procrastination has been mentioned in a hadith in which the Prophet ﷺ says: "Most of the pain of the people of hell will be because of procrastination." Even though this particular hadith has not been proven "authentic," its meaning is indeed authentic. God says: *As for those who will not believe in the life to come, they go on lying to themselves until, when death approaches any of them, he prays: "O my Sustainer! Let me return, let me return to life, so that I might act righteously in whatever I have neglected to do!" Nay* (Quran 23:99–100). Procrastination is unacceptable and is eventually regrettable. Every believer should seize time and make the best out of the time he has in this life.

And there is enough time to do almost everything one wishes to do. God will bless our time and work if we seize time and organise it. Time management is not only important for organising worldly affairs, but also for managing affairs with God. If you are in the habit of reciting a portion of the Quran or some *dhikr* (remembrance of God) every morning, and you have to leave early to work one day, seize the time while riding in the car, or while on the bus, or train, to recite the Quran, listen to it, or to simply reflect and mention God. I know of a number of brothers and sisters who memorised the whole Quran during their commutes on buses and trains. An average of one and a half hours every day allows you to memorise the whole Quran in a matter of two years!

People in developed countries usually read books or newspapers while on buses or trains. I lived five years in London and I remember how quiet London trains usually were. Even when they were crowded, they were very quiet because almost everyone was either reading, writing, or thinking, even if they were standing in the train! Believers should make the best use of their time for advancing their spiritual journey.

A believer should set his priorities straight and start with what is most important. According to the system of priorities in Islamic law, the rights of other people have higher priority than what scholars called "God's rights." This means that taking care of one's responsibilities towards other people should take precedence over pure acts of worship. However, this does not mean that we can neglect "God's rights." We should struggle to seize the time and strike a balance between the two kinds of rights.

EIGHTH STEP

Patience with tests

Do not be surprised when difficulties happen in this worldly abode. This is the nature of life.

IN THE NAME OF GOD, THE LORD OF GIVER, THE GIVER OF MERCY

If the servant of God repents to Him, relies on Him, purifies his intention to Him, reflects on Him, and seizes time, the light of faith will shine in his heart and his journey will draw him closer to God. As Ibn Ata said, "there is no real distance between you and Him in order for you to journey. And the connection between you and Him is not cut such that you must mend it."

The Prophet Muhammad mentioned that God said: "My servant continues to draw near to Me with additional work until I love him. When I love him, I am his hearing with which he hears, his sight with which he sees, his hand with which he strikes and his foot with which he walks. If he asks me, I will give him, and if he seeks my refuge, I will grant it to him."[12] "And if he draws near to Me a hand's span, I draw near to him an arm's length. And if he draws near to Me an arm's length, I draw near to him a fathom's length. And if he comes to Me walking, I go to him at speed."[13]

However, it is one of God's consistent and universal laws that when God loves someone, He will test him with trials in this world. God says: *Do people think that on their mere claiming, "We have attained to faith," they will be left to themselves, and will not be put to a test?* (Quran 29:2). A claim of belief has to be tested. God says: *And most certainly We shall try you all, so that We might mark out those of you who strive hard in Our cause and are patient in adversity: for We shall put to a test the truth of all your assertions* (Quran 47:31).

Trials vary but the response should be the same; patience and piety. *And most certainly shall We try you by means of danger, and hunger, and loss of worldly goods, of lives and of labour's fruits. But give glad tidings unto those who are patient in adversity* (Quran 2:155). *You shall most certainly be tried in your possessions and in your persons; and indeed you shall hear many hurtful things from those to whom revelation was granted before your time, as well as from those who have come to ascribe divinity to other beings beside God. But if you remain patient in adversity and pious—this, behold, is something to set one's heart upon* (Quran 3:186).

God announces that this worldly life is worth very little. So, if He deprives a person of this worldly life or part of it and guides him to repentance and bestows on him His mercy and Paradise instead, then this is, in fact, a great gift! Therefore, the Prophet ﷺ said: "The most severely tested people are the prophets, then the next best, then the next best. A man will be tested in accordance with his level of commitment to God."[14]

For this reason, if life is full of difficulties and challenges, one should not be surprised or ask why. It is as if Ibn Ata is asking us: What is the name of this world? The answer in Arabic is *al-dunya*, which literally means the lower life. Therefore, it is not surprising that difficult conditions, unpleasant events, and fatal consequences reveal themselves, because these things are derived from the very character and nature of this lower worldly life.

Accepting the nature of this worldly life helps the servant acquire a basic virtue and take a very important stop in his journey to God: patience with tests. Patience is a characteristic that delivers the servant into God's presence, as mentioned before: *God is with those who are patient in adversity* (Quran 2:153). And if we are in God's presence, then we need not worry.

Patience is of three types, namely, (1) patience in doing good, (2) patience in avoiding evil, and (3) patience with tests. Patience in doing good deeds means that the believer should be active continuously, without placing hardship on himself. God says: *God has laid no hardship on you in anything that pertains to religion* (Quran 22:78). The Prophet saw an old man walking, supported by his two sons, and asked about him. The people informed him that he had vowed to travel on foot to the Kaaba. The Prophet said: "God is not in need of this old man's torturing himself," and ordered him to get a ride to the Kaaba.[15] It is not "patience" to torture oneself or cause oneself harm.

As for patience in avoiding evil, it means that a believer should stay away from committing what God has forbidden. An example of this can be seen in the Quran, in the story of the Prophet Yusuf/ Joseph and one of the tests he was put to. *And it so happened that she in whose house he was living conceived a passion for him and sought to make him yield himself unto her; and she bolted the doors and said, "Come you unto me!" Joseph answered: "May God preserve me!"* (Quran 12:23).

There is a great reward for this type of patience in resisting physical desires. The Prophet ﷺ said that one of the seven persons whom God will give shade to on the Day when there would be no shade but that from Him is "a man whom a beautiful woman of high rank seduces for adultery, but he rejects by saying: I fear God.[16]

And patience with God's tests comes at different levels, all of which bear the meaning of refraining from something. The most basic level of patience with God's tests is to refrain from committing evil acts. Then, a higher level is to refrain from complaining by your tongue. Finally, the highest level of patience is to refrain even from complaining in your heart.

Refraining from committing sins is a condition for purifying one's heart. God says about the hypocrites: *Indeed, We tested them through suffering, but they did surrender to their Sustainer; and they will never humble themselves* (Quran 23:76). When a person faces some problems, then he is at a crossroads; either to repent and surrender to God, or to fall into sin, which means failing the test.

At a higher level, patience with God's tests requires one to refrain from even complaining about the test. This is called "beautiful patience," as God tells us about the story of Prophet Jacob ﷺ, when he said: *I will only show beautiful patience* (Quran 12:18), and *it is only to God that I complain of my deep grief and my sorrow* (Quran 12:86). The

Prophet Jacob ﷺ complained only to his Lord and refused to complain to anyone else.

Being patient with God's decree at the level of the heart is the best type of patience. The believer attains this degree when he not only refrains from speaking about the difficulty, but also refrains from agonizing about it in his heart. The soul is always at peace, even at the peak of crisis. The Prophet said: "Genuine patience is at the first stroke of a calamity."[17]

If the believer is patient in the face of tests, he will advance in the way of God. *Consider the flight of time! Verily, a human is bound to lose himself, unless he be of those who attain to faith, and do good works, and enjoin upon one another the keeping to truth, and enjoin upon one another patience in adversity* (Quran 103:1–3). And in any case, adversity does not last forever. *And, behold, with every hardship comes ease: verily, with every hardship comes ease!* (Quran 94:4–5).

NINTH STEP

Perfecting the beginnings

A sign of success in the end comes from relating [a matter] to God in the beginning. If there is no sunrise in the beginning, there is no sunrise in the end.

IN THE NAME OF GOD, THE LORD OF MERCY, THE GIVER OF MERCY

A servant journeying to God, who is passing through difficult tests and heading to horizons of peace and tranquillity always thinks of new good deeds that advance him along his journey. These words of wisdom teach us another universal law: Perfecting the basis and the start of any new project almost guarantees the desired outcomes in the end. In Ibn Ata's words, if there is a sunrise in the beginning, surely there will be a sunrise in the end. The question is, how can I make the sun rise and shine at the beginning? The answer, according to Ibn Ata, is by relating it to God. But, how could one "relate it to God" in the beginning of an act?

The Prophet Muhammad taught humanity something unique: how to start every daily action with a way of mentioning God that suits that action. The Prophet ﷺ said: "Every action that does not begin by invoking the praise of God is not blessed."[18] Therefore, start every action in the name of God. When giving a speech, start it by sending peace and blessings upon the Prophet and praising God Almighty. When starting an act of worship, start with a remembrance of pure intention. We are not required to begin the prayer by mentioning the intention to pray, but it is the Prophet's tradition to start the prayer with this supplication: "I turn my face in complete devotion to the One, the Originator of the heavens and the earth and I am not of the disbelievers."

And when embarking on significant tasks, pray two *rakat* (units of prayer) of *istikhara* (praying for the best course of action). All of these are ways of referring to God in the beginnings. *Istikhara* is a form of supplication to recite when you have a choice between two actions.

The Prophet Muhammad taught us the following supplication:

> "O God, I seek Your help in finding the best course of action in this matter by invoking Your knowledge; I ask You to empower me, and I beseech Your favour. You alone have absolute power, while I have no power. You alone know everything, while I do not. You are the One who knows the hidden mysteries. O God, if You know this thing I am embarking on [here mention your case] is good for me in my faith, worldly life, and my ultimate destiny, then facilitate it for me, and then bless me in my action. If You know this thing is detrimental for me in my faith, worldly life, and ultimate destiny, turn it away from me, and turn me away from it, and decree what is good for me, wherever it may be, and make me content with it."

The purpose of this supplication is to show that we wholeheartedly surrender to God and rely on Him alone. Seeking God's help is a kind of "referring to God in the beginnings," as Ibn Ata advised us. Therefore, it is a sign of success in its results, regardless of what these results are according to our human and worldly calculations of gain or loss. What matters is that we refer matters to God in the beginning so that the calculation will be in our favour in the end.

For example, if you are running a business trying to make a profit, there is a possibility that you may lose your investment. But if you pray *istikhara* and lose, think deeply about it. You might find that you lost some of your investment now, but that larger profits will follow in a different business in the future, after you learnt from the lessons of your loss. It is also possible that God made you lose so that you will reconsider many things, people, and plans in your life, which you examine in an effort to find out why you lost. You may continue to lose, but win a close friend who helped you during the time of your troubles. Therefore, your real success in the end may be from making a profit in another deal, reconsidering your plans, or even winning a friend. *God knows, whereas you do not know* (Quran 2:216).

The human standards of success and failure are usually based on financial calculations or figures, or some sort of "statistically verifiable" achievement. However, these calculations, in God's sight, and in reality, do not mean anything. What truly matters is God's pleasure in this life and the afterlife. So, if we refer to God in the beginning, the end will shine and God will be pleased, regardless of the material calculations.

This rule applies to everything. For example, the Prophet ﷺ said that one of the seven persons whom God would protect with His Shade on the Day when there would be no shade but that from Him is "a youth who grew up with the worship of God."[19] This young man or woman perfected the beginnings of their life; therefore God granted them success in the end and protected them under His Shade.

There will also be a sunrise in the beginning when one refrains from committing any sinful act and seeks to establish justice through all the affairs that he handles. On the contrary, if one commits forbidden acts in the beginning, surely the end will be a state of failure. *God does not further the works of those who spread corruption* (Quran 10:81). This is because doing the things that God made unlawful results in failure and obliterates blessings.

I pray to God to grant us happy and good endings. I also pray to God to help us refer to Him in every beginning so that we will achieve success in every end.

TENTH STEP

Discovering one's flaws

Attempting to discover the flaws within you is better than attempting to discover the spiritual worlds hidden from you.

IN THE NAME OF GOD, THE LORD OF MERCY, THE GIVER OF MERCY

One may start his journey to God the right way, but unfortunately, he may begin to feel conceited or think that he is doing God a favour and forget the fact that he has many flaws. After setting the rules of how to perfect the beginning of a new stage in the journey, Ibn Ata says: "Trying to discover the flaws within you is better than trying to discover the worlds hidden from you."

A believer who is active and has performed some extra acts of worship may feel a certain spiritual awakening. Then, he may think that he is able to feel or see the unseen or have the piercing sight about which the Prophet ﷺ said: "Beware of the piercing sight of the believer, for he sees with the light of God."[20] Therefore, Ibn Ata warns us by saying: "Attempting to discover the flaws within you is better than attempting to discover the spiritual worlds hidden from you."

If one thinks that he is free from flaws, then surely there is a problem. Flaws are part of the nature of human beings. Only God has the attributes of perfection, glory to Him. And as much perfection as God has, this is the imperfection we have. God is the Generous, while humans are misers: *Say: "If you were to own all the treasure-houses of my Sustainer's bounty, you would still try to hold on to them tightly for fear of spending: for man has always been avaricious, whereas God is limitless in His bounty* (Quran 17:100).

God is Almighty, while humans are weak creatures. *God wants to lighten your burdens: for man has been created weak* (Quran 4:28). God is always Merciful, while humans can be cruel. God is Most Forbearing, while humans have limited patience. God is All-Forgiving, while humans do not forgive easily. God is All-Wise, while humans are prone to hasty judgments. God is the Knower, while humans have very limited knowledge. God is the Just, while humans are often unjust.

In addition to these imperfections, at this stage of the journey we should strive to discover specific flaws within ourselves. This is much better than trying to discover the spiritual worlds hidden from us. One cannot have true insight into the spiritual world before purifying himself, in any case.

Know that a person can never purify himself completely, but he should do as much as he can. Trying to mend one's inner self eventually helps in realising the quality of humbleness. A certain degree of self-purification and humbleness elevate us and bring about divinely bestowed knowledge and spiritual insights.

1. There are Criticism: If someone criticises you, think about it. Could this criticism help reveal a flaw? Take into consideration every criticism that comes from everyone, even those people with whom you are not on good terms. Ask yourself, what can be learned from this?
2. Friends: A good friend helps to reveal flaws by offering sincere advice. Umar b. al-Khattab (may God be pleased with him) said: "May God have mercy on the person who bestows on me my flaws." Umar considered this act of revealing one of his flaws as a gift. A sincere friend comes to you directly and tells you about your flaws nicely. Listen carefully to your friend and look within yourself for those flaws and try to eliminate or decrease tTrials: Tests and trials will reveal your flaws and shortcomings. God says: *Are they, then, not aware that they are being tested year-in, year-out? And yet, they do not repent from or remember [their mistakes]* (Quran 9:126). The verse refers

to the hypocrites; God tests them, but they never repent to Him and they do not think of God. If you are under pressure or tested, you have an opportunity to discover your flaws.
3. We pray to God to help us discover and fix our flaws.

We pray to God to grant us forgiveness. He is the Most Generous.

ELEVENTH STEP

Self-criticism

The origin of every sin, forgetfulness, and lust is in being self-righteous, and the origin of every good deed, awareness, and chastity is in being self-critical.

IN THE NAME OF GOD, THE LORD OF MERCY, THE GIVER OF MERCY

After looking within ourselves and discovering our flaws, we must understand the origins of these flaws so that we can eliminate them. Thus, Ibn Ata says in this next step, "The origin of every sin, forgetfulness, and lust is in being self-righteous, and the origin of every good deed, awareness, and chastity is in being self-critical."

The origin of flaws in general—whether they are sins, forgetfulness or lusts—is a false sense of self-righteousness. Many people tell themselves: "I am really good! And I am doing good deeds too. Look at others. They are lost, but I am guided. They are evil and I am fine. I do not have to worry."

But God Almighty says: *Nay! I call to witness the Day of Resurrection! But nay! I call to witness the accusing voice of a human's own conscience!* (Quran 75:2). The accusing voice of a person's own conscience is something great enough for God to call as a witness! This is the inner voice of the believer who does not feel content with what he does and always blames himself.

In another verse we read: 2223*And yet, I am not trying to absolve myself: for, verily, one's inner self does incite to evil, and only they upon whom my Sustainer bestows His grace are saved. Behold, my Sustainer is All-Forgiving, a Dispenser of Grace!* (Quran 12:53). This self-critical statement from the Quran was spoken by Prophet Yusuf/Joseph ﷺ, and that is how he felt. What about us?

The voice of a person's own conscience will save him on the Day of Judgment. And a person who does not have a conscience to blame himself is in danger. In the Quranic story of the two owners of gardens, one of them was very content with himself. He even said: *And neither do I think that the Last Hour will ever come. But even if it should come, and I am brought before my Sustainer, I will surely find something even better than this as my last reward!* (Quran 18:36). He was confident that on the Day of Judgment, he will find a better garden than the one he had in this worldly life.

According to the Quran and the prophetic tradition, the default feeling of a believer should not be self-righteousness. This is what the Prophet ﷺ taught his Companions. Hanzala, one of the Prophet's Companions, had knowledge about the names of the ten hypocrites of Medina who were unknown to the other Companions. Umar b. al-Khattab used to ask Hanzala if his name was among the ten hypocrites! Why did Umar ask Hanzala this question? Clearly, he did this because he did not feel self-righteous at all. In fact, it shows a high level of self-criticism that is rare to find.

Abu Bakr al-Siddiq used to say: "I would not feel safe from God's deep devising even if one of my feet was in Paradise." Why did Abu Bakr say this? Because he thought that he does not deserve Paradise as a guaranteed reward from God. This is Abu Bakr, about whom the Prophet ﷺ said: "If the faith of Abu Bakr is put on one side of the scale and the faith of the nation of believers is put on the other side, the side of Abu Bakr will outweigh the other side."

A feeling of self-righteousness is the origin of all sins, Ibn Ata teaches us. If one feels self-righteous and think that he has secured an exclusive or special status, surely he will start to feel that he cannot make mistakes. But if you fear God and think that you are the least of the believers, you will avoid committing evil deeds.

In these words of wisdom Ibn Ata is also talking about the forbidden lusts of arrogance, miserliness, greed, extravagance, and so forth. He explains that the sense of self-righteousness is the origin of every forbidden lust. If we avoid this feeling, we will keep away from falling into these lusts. This was the practice of the prophets, messengers, and righteous people.

However, the virtue of self-criticism should not turn into self-destruction. Self-destruction happens when a person blames himself so harshly that he begins to feel desperate. For example, if a person continues to tell himself that he is no good, he has never done a sincere good deed, and so forth, he will eventually feel hopeless and abandon everything. This course of action is unacceptable.

Moderation and balance are virtues that lie between two vices; blaming oneself until one feels desperate and not blaming oneself at all until one becomes conceited. With moderation, our inner self will improve and we will advance in the course of our spiritual journey to God.

TWELFTH STEP

Good friends

Do not befriend someone who does not elevate you with his state, or guide you to God with his speech. It could be that you are doing evil, yet you think that you are doing good, because you are comparing yourself to your friend who is worse than you.

IN THE NAME OF GOD, THE LORD OF MERCY, THE GIVER OF MERCY

Throughout our journey to God we have learned how to search for our flaws. We have also learned that the origin of every sin, forgetfulness, and lust is in being self-righteous, and the origin of every good deed, awareness, and chastity is in being self-critical. Likewise, we have learned that one should be like the accusing voice of his conscience, which God called to witness in the Quran.

Here Ibn Ata teaches us about another serious flaw, the bad choice of friends. How should the believer choose his friends? Ibn Ata answers: "Do not befriend someone who does not elevate you with his state, or guide you to God with his speech. It could be that you are doing evil, yet you think that you are doing good, because you are comparing yourself to your friend who is worse than you."

You either befriend someone who is better than you or someone who is worse than you. Ibn Ata says that when you befriend someone who is worse than you, you will think that you are being excellent in any case. But this is only because you are comparing yourself to your friend, who is a person with minor or major faults and does not care. However, if you befriend someone who elevates you with his state, or guides you to God with his speech; that is, someone who is better than you in terms of faith, this friend will have a good influence on you.

The Prophet ﷺ is reported to have said; "A good friend and a bad friend are like a perfume-seller and a blacksmith: The perfume-seller might give you some perfume as a gift, or you might buy some from him, or at least you might smell its fragrance. As for the blacksmith, he might burn your clothes, and at the very least you will breathe in the fumes of his furnace."[21]

If you befriend someone who is of a good character, he may give you some amount of perfume; a believer always has a good smell. He might also give you perfume in a moral sense, in the form of a piece of advice, reminder, Quranic wisdom, good guidance, or even a smile. The Prophet ﷺ said: "Smiling in the face of your brother is charity."[22] He might be a good example for you when you see him give charity, say a good word, or pray to God. You will find yourself participating with him in his good deeds.

The other person, who is like the blacksmith, might burn your clothes if he smokes! And if you get close to him, he may burn your heart by involving you in backbiting, gossip, false testimony, and other evil actions.

"Do not befriend someone who does not elevate you with his state." A "state" is a Sufi expression for the spiritual influence that people have on one's spirituality. This influence has been explained by the Prophet ﷺ in different traditions. The Prophet said: "One dirham has become greater than a hundred thousand dirhams." The Companions asked: "How can that be, O Messenger of God?" He replied, "A rich man takes a hundred thousand dirhams from his wealth and gives it away as charity. Another man has nothing except two dirhams, and so he takes one dirham and gives it away in charity."[23] Here, the only difference between the two men is in the "state" of their hearts, even though the second man gave one hundred thousand more dirhams!

It is reported that the Prophet performed the *fajr* (dawn) prayer and he read the Surat al-Rum and he became confused in the recitation. When he finished the prayer, he said: "What about people who pray with us while they do not know how to perform their ablution. We became confused in the recitation of the Quran because of them."[24] This hadith is about the "state" of an individual; a state that negatively affected the whole congregation praying behind the Prophet ﷺ.

Jubayr b. Mutim reported, I heard the Prophet reciting Surat al-Tur in the *maghrib* (sunset) prayer, and when he reached the verse: *Or do they deny the existence of God? Have they themselves been created without anything that might have caused their creation? or were they, perchance, their own creators? And have they created the heavens and the earth? Nay, but they have no certainty of anything! How could they? Are your Sustainer's treasures with them? Or are they in charge of destiny?* (Quran 52:35–37), Jubayr said: When I heard this, my heart was about to fly![25]

Ubayy b. Kab reported, I was in the mosque when a man entered and prayed and recited (the Quran) in a style to which I objected. Then another man entered (the mosque) and recited in a style different from that of his companion. When we had finished the prayer, we all went to God's Messenger and said to him: This man recited in a style to which we objected, and the other entered and recited in a style different from that of his companion. The Messenger of God asked them to recite and so they recited, and the Messenger of God expressed approval of all their different recitations! There occurred in my mind a sort of denial which has never occurred to me even during the Days of Ignorance before Islam. When the Messenger of God saw how I was affected, he struck my chest gently, whereupon I broke into a sweat and felt as though I were looking at God with fear.[26]

It is as if the Prophet blamed Ubayy for doubting the authenticity of the Quran, just because it could be read in different Arabic dialects. Ubayy eventually became one of the members of the committee that wrote down the whole Quran when it was later collected in one book during the time of the third caliph. When the Prophet struck his chest, Ubayy's state changed from that of doubt to that of excellence; "to worship God as though you are seeing Him, and while you see Him not yet truly He sees you." When Ubayy said, "as though I were looking at God with fear," he was describing the state to which the Prophet moved him in a moment. The state of the Prophet himself ﷺ is the secret behind his ability to change the state of Ubayy.

I have witnessed this in some of my teachers, whose one-word comment on something could elevate my "state" for days. On certain occasions, some may not even speak at all, yet they influenced me deeply with a high state of remembering God that they were experiencing.

Then Ibn Ata says: "And does not guide you to God with his speech." This is the next level of friends; a friend who does not necessarily elevate you with his state, but guides you to God with his words.

THIRTEENTH STEP

Perseverance in the remembrance of God

Do not stop mentioning God just because your heart is not present. Forgetting Him completely is worse than being inattentive while you are mentioning Him; perhaps He will elevate you from being inattentive to being attentive, and from being attentive to being fully present with Him, and from being fully present with Him to being fully absent from anything but Him. This is not difficult for God *(Quran 35:17).*

IN THE NAME OF GOD, THE LORD OF MERCY, THE GIVER OF MERCY

Along the path of our journey, we progress through stages, purification, searching for our flaws, and attempting to get rid of them. These words of wisdom tackle a serious flaw of the soul, "forgetfulness"; that is, the lack of the remembrance of God. We often fall into this error throughout the day, and the solution is to remember God, with our tongues or in our hearts.

God says *And remember your Sustainer humbly and with awe, and without raising your voice, in the mornings and in the evenings; and do not allow yourself to be heedless* (Quran 7:205), *remember Him as the One who guided you* (Quran 2:198), *bear God in mind—since it is He who taught you what you did not previously know* (Quran 3:239), *and when you have finished your prayer, remember God—standing and sitting and lying down* (Quran 4:103), *O you who have attained to faith! Remember God with unceasing remembrance. And extol His limitless glory from morn to evening* (Quran 33:41–42), *so remember Me, and I shall remember you* (Quran 2:152). The Prophet ﷺ said: "Always keep your tongue busy with God's remembrance."[27] These are clear directions to remember God in all times and in every situation. The Prophet used to mention God in all situations, and for every situation he had a special supplication, which is in itself a form of mentioning God.

Mentioning God brings about a state of rest in the heart and this draws one closer to God. We read in the Quran: *Those who believe, and whose hearts find their rest in the remembrance of God—for, verily, in the remembrance of God hearts do find their rest* (Quran 13:28). Mentioning God is the ultimate goal of any act of worship. God says: *and be constant in prayer, so as to remember Me!* (Quran 20:14). This means that the objective of the prayer itself is God's remembrance. And God's remembrance is even greater than prayer in terms of restraining ourselves from evil. God says: *behold, prayer restrains people from loathsome deeds and from all that runs counter to reason; but remembrance of God is indeed the greatest good* (Quran 29:45).

Ibn Ata assumes that we mention God's name all the time, and is addressing the problem of not feeling that remembrance in our hearts. Should I stop God's remembrance when I do not feel it in my heart? Or should I continue with God's remembrance despite that?

Ibn Ata says: "Do not stop mentioning God just because your heart is not present. Forgetting Him completely is worse than being inattentive while you are mentioning Him; perhaps He will elevate you from being inattentive to being attentive, and from being attentive to being fully present with Him, and from being fully present with Him to being fully absent from anything but Him." *This is not difficult for God.*

This means that if your heart is not present when you mention God, do not stop mentioning God. This is the case when, for example, you are reading the Quran but cannot reflect on the verses you are reading because your mind is so busy with something else. It is also the case when you recite the regular *dhikr,* but do not feel the meanings of *subhana Allah* (glory be to God), *al-hamdullilah* (praise be to God), or *la illaha illa Allah* (there is not god but God). Here the shaykh says that in such cases, do not stop mentioning God.

Ibn Ata explains: Forgetting Him completely is worse than being inattentive while you are mentioning Him. The least degree of mentioning God is when you mention Him while you are inattentive, but at least you know what you are saying. Recall the verse in which God says: *O you who have attained to faith! do not attempt to pray while you are in a state of drunkenness, but wait until you know what you are saying* (Quran 4:43). Perhaps, and God is Most Generous, He will elevate you from being inattentive to being attentive. If you continue, hoping that God will change your inattentiveness, He will elevate you to the state of being attentive. Then, if you continue, He might raise you to an even higher state of heart.

Ibn Ata says: "Perhaps He will elevate you from being attentive to being fully present with Him." Being fully present with Him is a degree higher than being attentive, that is, the servant's heart is present while mentioning God. This means that when you mention Paradise, you call it to your mind, and when you mention God, you call to your mind His glory and favours. And so on.

This presence of the heart is what Ali b. Abi Talib (may God be pleased with him) described in his famous sermon about the characteristics of those who are conscious of God. Imam Ali said: "When they come across a verse that inspires awe they bend the ears of their hearts towards it, and feel as though the sound of hell and its cries are reaching their ears. If they come across a verse creating eagerness for Paradise, they pursue it avidly, and their spirits turn towards it eagerly, and they feel as if it is right there in front of them." This is being attentive.

It is not difficult for God to elevate us from being inattentive to being attentive, and from being attentive to being fully present with Him. If we are elevated to such a level, we will be like the Companions who felt and heard the unseen world of Paradise and Hell.

Then, Ibn Ata talks about a very special state of heart. He says: "Then God will elevate you from being fully present with Him to being fully absent from anything but Him." This is a heart that mentions God and does not feel anything around it. This is a heavenly favour which, if bestowed on any believer once a day or twice a week, he will be most blessed. There is a difference between deep intellectual reflection upon God, and being emotionally absent from anything but God, even for a moment.

To give one example, this is the state that made someone like Abdullah b. al-Zubayr, the great Companion, not sense the falling of one of the walls of his house while he was praying. In fact, during his prayers, birds landed on the top of his head, thinking that they were landing on a tree! After his prayers, he was asked why he did not leave the prayers and avoid the danger, and his reply was that he did not even hear a sound!

This high state, however, has nothing to do with those who claim that they are nothing but God, and that they are not part of this world, etc. This is too much of an exaggeration.

Finally, Ibn Ata quotes the verse, *this is not difficult for God* (Quran 35:17). The context of that verse in its chapter is the following: *O people! It is you who stand in need of God, whereas He alone is self-sufficient, the One to whom all praise is due. If He so wills, He can do away with you and bring forth a new creation: this is not difficult for God* (Quran 35:15–17). Let us hope that, out of God's mercy and generosity, He will do away with our forgetful selves and bring forth a new creation in us; a creation that mentions Him deeply and fully. We learned from the first word of wisdom that we must not rely on our good actions and we must put our trust in His mercy alone.

FOURTEENTH STEP

Freedom from humiliation, neediness, and illusion

The tree of humiliation stems from a seed of neediness. Nothing deceives as much as illusion. You are free from what you give up, and you are a slave to what you need.

IN THE NAME OF GOD, THE LORD OF MERCY, THE GIVER OF MERCY

Purifying the heart to allow for beautification and illumination is still part of the process of searching for flaws. Trying to discover the flaws within you is better than trying to discover the worlds hidden from you, as mentioned before.

One of the flaws that the Shaykh explains here is "humiliation." One might ask: How can humiliation be my fault and not the fault of the people who humiliated me? The answer is that suffering from humiliation is one's own fault! The Shaykh explains that the direct reason for being humiliated by people is the neediness in one's heart towards the people. Ibn Ata eloquently expresses this in the following words: "The tree of humiliation (by people) stems from a seed of neediness (to them)." A seed of the feeling of being in need of people grows into a tree of humiliation. This tree is watered with words and actions, through which the needy beg for what they want from people, and thus end up in a state of humiliation. Neediness makes you a slave to others, not to God.

But what is the reason behind my neediness? It is my "illusion." Ibn Ata says: "Nothing deceives as much as illusion. You are free from what you give up, and you are a slave to what you are in need of." The one who is need of what people have might think that those people will actually benefit or harm him, and this is an illusion. The real One who benefits or harms you is your Lord.

Out of illusion, one might think that people who have power or wealth, for example, will bring benefit or harm to him. Thus, one allows himself to be humiliated by the people he is in need of. In fact, people never bring benefit or cause harm to others. Neediness is the source of humiliation, and illusion is the source of neediness. Freedom from all of this is the solution and is another step in God's way.

It is true that one must interact with people, ask them for help or a favour. There is nothing wrong with this as long as seeking peoples' help does not bring with any neediness in one's heart, which in turn produces humiliation and servitude. It is all about the feeling of neediness or humiliation in the heart; this is the flaw that the Shaykh advises us to eliminate.

The Prophet ﷺ says: "Ask for your needs with dignity." It is normal to ask for your needs, but when you ask people to do you a favour or ask them for money, you must ask them with dignity—without begging or feeling humiliated. Do not plant the seed of neediness in your heart, or it will lead to humiliation that grows like a tree, God forbid, and eventually, humiliation transforms us into slaves to others than God.

If you free yourself from the illusion that people have the ability to benefit or harm you, you will be saved, and you will deal with people with the right state of heart. The Prophet ﷺ gave Ibn Abbas (may God be pleased with him) the following advice, and Ibn Abbas at that time was a young boy. The Prophet said: "O young lad! Know that if the whole nation were to unite and try to benefit you with something, they would never benefit you except by that which God has written for you. And if the whole nation were to unite and try to harm you with something, they would never be able to harm you except with that which God had written for you."[28]

Real freedom comes from servitude to God. This is the definition of freedom in the Islamic worldview. And if you are a true servant of God, then you are free from other than Him. You are free from human beings, material things, and even from your own desires. You are free from any social, political, psychological, or financial pressure. You are free from all this because "you gave up on them," as Ibn Ata so eloquently puts it. You have no illusion, no neediness, and no humiliation, and you have your freedom.

Finally, these precious words of wisdom can be understood from another perspective. Consider the following additions between brackets: The tree of servitude (to God) stems from a seed of neediness (to God). Nothing deceives you as your illusion (that you are not in need of God). You are free from what you gave up (which is the "others"), and you are a slave to what you are in need of (who is your Lord).

Let us also work on nurturing the tree of servitude and the sense of neediness to God alone, and let us give up on "others." This will lead us to the next step on our journey.

FIFTEENTH STEP

Thanking God for His blessings

You risk losing your blessings when you do not thank Him for them, and you tie them to you firmly when you do. And if you do not advance towards Him by doing excellent deeds, He will pull you towards Him with the chain of tests.

IN THE NAME OF GOD, THE LORD OF MERCY, THE GIVER OF MERCY

One of the universal laws of God which governs the issue of providence in all its forms is the reality that if we thank God, He will multiply the blessings or replace them with something better. God says: *If you are grateful [to Me], I shall most certainly give you more and more* (Quran 14:7).

God declared that we will not be able to count all God's blessings. God says: *and should you try to count God's blessings, you could never compute them* (Quran 14:34). Every Muslim should do his best to thank God for whatever He gives him.

Then God says: *but if you are ungrateful (kafartum), verily, My chastisement will be severe indeed!* (Quran 14:7). In this verse, the Arabic word *kafartum*, means being unthankful to God for His blessings. It does not mean disbelief in God, as the literal meaning implies, but it shows the gravity of this flaw. Lack of gratitude then, is another flaw that Ibn Ata teaches us in these words of wisdom.

Ibn Ata says: "You risk losing your blessings when you do not thank Him for them, and you tie them to you firmly when you do." The one who thanks God for His blessings, is tying them to him firmly. God's promise to reward those who thank Him is a true promise. It is a guarantee for the continuation of your blessings, or more. It does come with one condition, however, which is to thank God for these blessings.

Thankfulness is not limited to saying *al-hamdullilah* (praise to God), it can be offered through action. God says: *Labour, O David's people, in gratitude towards Me* (Quran 34:13). Thankfulness through action requires that everyone ask himself, what am I going to do with this blessing? Am I going to use it in a good way? Am I going to contribute with it to good causes? Or am I going to waste it—and this is a form of denying the blessing.

Therefore, if you do not thank God for His blessings with words and actions, you risk losing them. But if you thank God, you are tying His blessings to you firmly.

Then the Shaykh says: "And if you do not advance towards Him by doing excellent deeds, He will pull you towards Him with the chain of tests." Thus, if you do not thank God for His blessings and advance to Him until you reach the level of excellence, God will test you. By giving you tests, God offers you a chance to reach the level of excellence. This is also a universal law.

Through tests, God elevates you and purifies your heart. When you are afflicted with tests, you draw closer to God and He forgives your sins. God says: *And, indeed, We tested them [the hypocrites] through suffering, but they did not abase themselves before their Sustainer; and they will never humble themselves* (Quran 23:76). When God gives you tests, you humble yourself, and pray to God. God also says about the hypocrites: *Are they, then, not aware that they are being tested year-in, year-out? And yet, they do not repent and do not bethink themselves [of God]* (Quran 9:126).

God does not test you to punish you. He wants to draw you closer to Him and to make you count the blessings which He bestows on you. He wants you to thank Him with your words and actions.

When God tests you by removing some blessings, He is testing you with a "touch of chastisement," as the other verse says. Every one of us has billions of uncountable blessings. When God puts one of us to a test by losing one, two, or even five blessings, we feel that we are faced with a severe crisis. While in reality we have billions of blessings which God bestows on us every moment.

In every cell in our bodies there are countless blessings. In every second we live, there are countless blessings. In every breath we breathe, there are countless blessings. In every glance, there are countless blessings. God is the One who is worthy of thankfulness. When God tests us by removing one or two blessings, according to Ibn Ata, He is "pulling you towards Him." By losing a blessing, God wants us to return and repent to Him. He also wants us to remember His blessings and reflect on them.

And if you sincerely repent to God, the test is over. God says: *And, behold, with every hardship comes ease: verily, with every hardship comes ease!* (Quran 94:5–6). God repeats the verse twice. In another verse we read: *God will grant, after hardship, ease* (Quran 65:7). Sometimes matters get worse, but God makes a way out and with difficulty comes ease. When you are faced with a problem or afflicted with a calamity, God brings ease in the middle of the crisis and also after the crisis. And, when the state of hardship draws you closer to God, this is, in itself, a blessing from God.

If we want to avoid trials at all, we must continuously advance towards God and never fall into error. In reality, this cannot happen because we are human! We cannot maintain a clear record, thanking God all the time. The Prophet ﷺ said: "Every son of Adam makes mistakes, but the best of those who make mistakes are those who repent."[29] God helps us in our journey by testing us, in order to give us a chance to repent.

SIXTEENTH STEP

Understanding God's giving and depriving

You might think that He is giving you (something), while in reality He is depriving you! And you might think that He is depriving you, while in reality He is giving you (something)! If through your deprivation, He opens the doors of understanding for you, then this deprivation is a gift. You feel that your deprivation is dreadful because you do not understand. He might open the door of worship for you, but does not open the door of acceptance. And you might be destined to sin, but this becomes a means of ascension towards Him. A sin that produces humbleness and need is better than an act of worship that produces arrogance and prejudice.

IN THE NAME OF GOD, THE LORD OF MERCY, THE GIVER OF MERCY

At times God gives and at other times He deprives. God might test us through "good" and "bad," through "fortune" and "hardship," or through bestowing "blessings" on us or "depriving" us from them. But the reality of each of the above could turn out to be different from the way we label it and the assumptions we make about it.

At this stage in our journey to God, Ibn Ata teaches us the importance of forming a deep understanding of the wisdom behind God's "giving" and "depriving." God says: *But as for a human, whenever his Sustainer tries him by His generosity and by letting him enjoy a life of ease, he says, "My Sustainer has been generous towards me"; whereas, whenever He tries him by tightening his means of livelihood, he says, "My Sustainer has disgraced me!" But nay* (Quran 89:15-17). "Nay" here means that this is not a correct understanding of having "a life of ease" or "tight means."

Here God says that when He tries us by tightening our means of livelihood, this does not mean that He is disgracing us. And when

He tries us by letting us enjoy a life of ease for a while, this is not necessarily good. The question is, how can we judge?

The Shaykh draws our attention to the very important meaning of these words of wisdom—that of "understanding" (*fahm*): "If through your deprivation, He opens the doors of understanding for you, then this deprivation is a gift." And this is how we judge. If God deprives us and we lose some of our wealth, opportunity, health, or family, and at the same time, He opens the doors of "understanding," then this is not deprivation. It is a gift. In this case, the trial is a gift.

Before forming the correct "understanding," we were looking at the material level only, at the level of the five senses, and the numbers and figures. For example, if I say I lost ten thousand dollars or I lost my health: this is a material calculation at the material level.

But God might take ten thousand dollars and give me the ability to understand, a feeling of contentment, a good deed, a strong will, a good friend, and closeness to Him, on top of all that. Thus, my loss of ten thousand dollars becomes, actually, a gift. It is even possible that God will give me a hundred thousand dollars later, if I work hard and try to learn from my lessons.

We must understand the actual meaning of giving and deprivation. Sometimes, we think that a specific thing is a deprivation while it is the actual giving, and vice versa. A person might earn a large amount of money, for example, but not thank God in word or by actions. This might continue and he might waste his money in evil ways. Then, God may even give this person more wealth and opportunities to return to Him. God says: *for, behold, though I may give them rein for a while, My subtle scheme is exceedingly firm!* (Quran 68:45). *Then, when they had forgotten all that they had been told to take to heart, We threw open to them the gates of all good things until—even as they were rejoicing in what they had been granted—We suddenly took them to task: and lo! they were broken in spirit; and in the end, the last remnant of those folk who had been bent on evildoing was wiped out. For all praise is due to God, the Sustainer of all the worlds* (Quran 6:44–45).

If God opens the doors of providence for you or grants you a request, He is calling you, as the Shaykh said, to understand. First, thank God so that the blessing is tied to you. Second, reflect upon the wisdom and the meaning behind this giving and be cautious about the trial it might involve.

The Shaykh gives two specific examples. He says: "He might open the door of worship for you, but does not open the door of acceptance. And you might be destined to sin, but this becomes a means to ascension towards Him."

God might open doors for you and you find yourself doing some good, such as praying, memorising the Quran, giving in charity, fasting, performing hajj, attending a course, teaching people, or leading them in the way of religion. But be cautious. Sometimes you imagine that worship is in itself a gift from God, but in reality it is not. Why? Because one might perform the action and miss the reward.

God says: *They who spend their possessions for the sake of God and do not thereafter mar their spending by stressing their own benevolence and hurting the feelings of the needy shall have their reward with their Sustainer* (Quran 2:262). Here is an example of a good deed, charity, which is marred and rendered void by another action, such as hurting the feelings of the needy. This later action nullifies the charity and closes the door of acceptance and heavenly reward.

Some people do good, only to show off and be praised by people, thus leading themselves to punishment. *Behold, the hypocrites seek to deceive God—while it is He who causes them to be deceived by themselves. And when they rise to pray, they rise reluctantly, only to be seen and praised by people, remembering God but seldom* (Quran 4:142). The main purpose of an act of worship is sincerity and gaining moral and spiritual benefit from it. A ritual devoid of sincerity and moral and spiritual benefit is worthless. The Prophet Muhammad ﷺ said: "Whoever does not give up forged speech and evil actions, God is not in need of his leaving food and drink in fasting." This means that God will not accept his fasting, which looks like a good deed while it is not.

Another example from the Shaykh relates to the issue of acts of worship and sinning, and requires an accurate understanding. The Shaykh says: "And you might be destined to sin, but this becomes a means of ascension towards Him." Imam Ibn Qayyim al-Jawziyya says something similar in this regard: "A sin may produce humbleness and need so that it takes one to Paradise. An act of worship may produce pride and prejudice so that it takes one to hell."

Of course, sinning itself does not lead one to enter Paradise. But if the sin already happened and the person who committed it repents sincerely to God, it might be good, in the larger picture. This is true if the person repents, changes his ways, and always remembers his sin with grief and tries his best to compensate with good deeds. In this case, sinning that produces humbleness and need becomes a gift from God, in the long term.

But this does not mean that one should commit a sin and say that I am sinning in order to eventually be humble and repent to God. This is a wrong and deviant understanding that was unfortunately adopted by some ignorant people who claimed to be Sufis.

On the other hand, an act of worship that produces arrogance in one's heart is an evil deed, not a good one. The Prophet ﷺ said: "He who has in his heart the weight of a mustard seed of arrogance shall not enter Paradise."

These matters depend on our response. The Prophet ﷺ said: "How wonderful is the affair of the believer, for his affairs are all good, and this applies to no one but the believer. If something good happens to him, he is thankful for it and that is good for him. If something bad happens to him, he bears it with patience and that is good for him." This hadith indicates that we are the ones who bring good or bad outcomes to ourselves. It is all up to us! If we are thankful to God for the good things that happen, this is good for us. If we are patient when bad things happen to us, this is also good for us. However, if we are arrogant when good things happen, this is an evil outcome. If we are impatient when bad things happen, this is also an evil outcome. Thus, based on our reactions, we determine whether what happens to us is a heavenly gift or otherwise.

But God always chooses what is best for people, and it is up to them to decide how they receive God's choices. *In Your hand, God, is all good. Verily, You have the power to will anything* (Quran 3:26).

SEVENTEENTH STEP

Enjoying God's company and praying to Him
If He takes you away from people, then know that He is opening to you the doors of His company. And if He allows you to ask, then know that He wants to give you something.

IN THE NAME OF GOD, THE LORD OF MERCY, THE GIVER OF MERCY

These words of wisdom are another example related to understanding God's giving and depriving. The Shaykh says: "If He takes you away from people, then know that He is opening to you the doors of His company." Sometimes God may test us with the death of a spouse, a brother, or a dear person. We might find ourselves travelling to a remote country for one reason or another. We might find ourselves in jail, God forbid, or suddenly alone in a hospital. In all these cases, we may feel lonely and isolated. Yet, this could be another step in our journey to God!

The Shaykh makes it clear that all such trials might be gifts from God in the form of trials. There are unconfirmed reports in which the Prophet says: "If God wishes to benefit someone, He will take him away from people." The meaning of this hadith may be true in light of the wisdom discussed here. When you feel lonely, God is opening a door of uninterrupted remembrance and meditation. Being in His company is something that you might not be able to feel if you are a person who mixes with people all the time, day and night. You might think that isolation is a trial, whereas in reality it is a gift.

One of my teachers often recalls some stages of his life which he spent in jail and says: "If it were not for that jail, I would not have written most of my books or developed most of my ideas."

Thus, imprisonment and loneliness were a reason for being in God's company and benefiting people with his knowledge. This is a gift.

Then the Shaykh says: "And if He allows you to ask, then know that He wants to give you something." This means that God may test you with something so difficult that there is no solution except to pray to God. Perhaps before that time of trial, you did not pray sincerely enough to God. You might have thought that you were not in need of prayer or distress. Yet, when a serious crisis comes and the only solution is God's help, then prayers are much deeper and more sincere. *Who is it that responds to the distressed when he calls out to Him?* (Quran 27:62).

Praying to God may continue for days or weeks without an apparent end to your trials. This could be another precious gift from God, not because of your deprivation, but because of your continuous state of worship. The Prophet ﷺ said: "Supplication is the true worship."[30]

But the Shaykh says: "And if He allows you to ask, then know that He wants to give you something." God gives abundant rewards just for praying to Him. Not only that, but He answers those who pray to Him, either in this world or the next, or both. Therefore, God allows us to ask because He wants to give us something. If you ask a generous person for help, surely he will answer you. What about if you ask God Himself!

Deprivation and giving should not be measured by human standards, which are based on material gains. The true standard is our relation with God. Sometimes God puts you to a test and after God removes the affliction your relation with Him improves. This is in itself a gift from God.

EIGHTEENTH STEP

Ascending in the levels of worship

God diversified the acts of worship because He knows how quickly you become weary. And He did not permit you certain acts of worship at certain times so you do not go to extremes. The objective is to perfect your prayers, not to merely perform them. Not every performer of prayers perfects them.

IN THE NAME OF GOD, THE LORD OF MERCY, THE GIVER OF MERCY

The words of wisdom discussed here relate to a very important topic in our journey to God—the quality of worship. A believer who worships continuously may feel weary at some point. God, out of His mercy, knows that we humans, could naturally feel weary, even in worship. Therefore, He diversified the acts of worship so that we can worship God in a variety of ways.

For example, prayer is a fixed act of worship that must be performed five times a day. But God recommended other forms of supererogatory prayers, such as the late-night prayer, the prayer of thankfulness, and prayer in times of need, and so forth. If the believer is weary from (optional) prayers, he may perform the obligatory prayers only, but at the same time he may involve himself in other forms of worship, such as charity, performing *umra*, seeking knowledge, being kind to neighbours and relatives, helping people, and so forth. All these are forms of worship that draw one closer to God.

People are different, and diversity is a universal law of God. Diversity is not limited to natural capabilities only, but there is diversity in one's ability to keep up with certain actions and enjoy them. Here the Shaykh is also referring to God's knowledge about our desire to continue our worship without a pause. In His infinite knowledge, He prohibited some acts of worship at certain times. As mentioned before, the Prophet ﷺ said: "Surely this religion is firm. So apply it with tenderness. The traveller who is too harsh on his riding animal will not reach his destination and the riding animal will die." This is why the Prophet recommended that we do not pray right after the sunrise, right before noon time, or in the late afternoon after the *asr* prayer. The wisdom behind not praying any recommended prayer in these times is to make us eager to perform them when we are allowed. The same applies to fasting. We are not permitted to fast at certain times, for example, immediately before the beginning of Ramadan or on the first day of Eid.

When God opens for you the door of reading the Quran, you may wish to read it all the time. But we are not allowed to read the Quran while kneeling down or prostrating in prayer, in the bathroom, or while we are in a state of impurity. Because God knows our nature, He diversified the acts of worship and prohibited them at certain times.

Then, when God guides you to perform an act of worship, perfect it and ascend in the levels of quality of worship. The Shaykh gives the example of prayer, when he says: "The objective is to perfect your prayers, not to merely perform them. Not every performer of prayer perfects them." When God talks about prayer in the Quran, he asked us to *establish prayers* (Quran 2:43). Establishing the prayer is different from merely performing it. Establishing the prayer is about concentration and humbleness during the prayer. God says: *Truly, to a happy state shall attain the believers, those who humble themselves in their prayer* (Quran 23:1–2). Humbleness is the objective of avoiding the performance of prayer at certain times. If one feels weary, or goes to extremes and prays non-stop, humbleness cannot be achieved.

According to Sufis, humbleness in prayers (*khushu*) is a branch of knowledge. This is supported by the prophetic tradition in which the Prophet ﷺ talked about the signs of the Day of Judgment, as reported by Abu al-Darda: "We were with the Prophet. He looked at the sky and said: This is a time when knowledge is abandoned by people so that they cannot do anything. Then he said: If you want, I can tell you about the first branch of knowledge that will be abandoned by people; it is humbleness in prayers. You may enter a big mosque but you do not see one man in a state of humbleness."[31]

In fact, scholars divide humbleness in prayers into three levels; humiliation, awe, and happiness.

The first level is humiliation. This means that we pray to God and feel humiliated before Him. This is reflected in the movements of the prayer. We kneel down and prostrate only to God. These movements are a manifestation of humiliation, which should be shown only to God. Humiliation requires that we feel our weakness and sense that God is the Powerful, the Rich, and the Almighty. Humiliation is the result of neediness, as the Shaykh explained before, when he said: "The tree of humiliation stems from a seed of neediness." When we feel we are in need of God, a state of humbleness is produced.

The second level is awe of God. The higher level is to elevate us from the stage of humiliation to the stage of feeling awe of God and His Might. God says: *whenever the messages of the Most Gracious were conveyed unto them [the prophets], they would fall down before Him, prostrating themselves and weeping* (Quran 19:58). This is the level of feeling awe of God, a level that sometimes leads to crying. *God bestows from on high the best of all teachings in the shape of a divine writ fully consistent within itself, repeating each statement [of the truth] in manifold forms [a divine writ] whereat shiver the skins of all who stand in awe of their Sustainer: [but] in the end their skins and their hearts do soften at the remembrance of [the grace of] God. Such is God's guidance: He guides therewith him that wills [to be guided] whereas he whom God lets go astray can never find any guide* (Quran 39:23). One of the Companions reported that he watched the Prophet ﷺ as he was praying. He said that he heard a whistling sound from the chest of the Prophet resembling the sound of a boiling kettle as he was weeping.[32]

The third level is happiness. The best state of humbleness in prayer is happiness and pleasure being in the presence of God. This feeling of happiness and elation when reading the Quran, mentioning God or praising Him is the highest level of humbleness in prayers. Angels descend from the heavens to listen and a state of tranquillity prevails in the area.

It is reported that while Usayd b. Hudayr was reciting Surat al-Baqara (the second chapter of the Quran) at night, and his horse was tied beside him, the horse was suddenly startled and troubled. When he stopped reciting, the horse became quiet, and when he started again, the horse was startled again. Then he stopped reciting and the horse became quiet too. He started reciting again and the horse was startled and troubled once again. Then he stopped reciting and his son, Yahya was beside the horse. He was afraid that the horse might trample on him. When he took the boy away and looked towards the sky, he could not see it. All he saw was a low cloud full of lamps! The next morning he informed the Prophet, who said, "Recite, O Ibn Hudayr! Recite, O Ibn Hudayr!" Ibn Hudayr replied, "O God's Messenger! My son, Yahya was near the horse and I was afraid that it might trample on him, so I looked towards the sky, and went to him. When I looked at the sky, I saw something like a cloud containing what looked like lamps, so I went out in order not to see it." The Prophet said, "Do you know what that was?" Ibn Hudayr replied, "No." The Prophet said, "Those were angels who came near you for your voice and if you had kept on reciting till dawn, it would have remained there till morning when people would have seen it as it would not have disappeared."[33]

Al-Bara reported that a person was reciting Surat al-Kahf and there was a horse tied with two ropes at his side, a cloud overshadowed him, and as it began to come nearer and nearer his horse began to take fright from it. He went and mentioned this to the Prophet ﷺ in the morning, and the Prophet said: "That was Tranquillity. It came down at the recitation of the Quran."[34]

Bear in mind, however, that when God takes you to a level of happiness in your prayers, this will be out of His Grace, not because of your deeds. A poem in Arabic says:

> In the twinkling of an eye.
> God may change everything.
> From one state to another.

However, there are means that one could follow in order to ascend to that level, by God's grace. Among these is to reflect upon the meaning of the Quran, and develop humbleness by calling to mind God's greatness.

The three levels mentioned above may be expressed in various forms of worship, not only in prayer. The level of submission (*islam*) to God is the outward work. In prayers, it is performing the motions of the prayers by standing, kneeling down, and prostrating. In charity, it is giving money. In fasting, it is abstaining from eating and drinking. In pilgrimage, it is circumambulating around the Kaaba, going between the two hills of Safa and Marwa, and offering the sacrifice.

The level of belief (*iman*) is the work of the heart. The basic work of the heart is to believe in God, His angels, His scriptures, His messengers, the Day of Judgment, and God's creation of all things to come, good or bad. All this gives a wider meaning to the rituals. Prayer is not only about kneeling down and prostrating, it is also about humbleness, feeling awe of God, and happiness. Charity is not merely the act of giving money, it is about having mercy upon the poor and being indifferent to the world. Fasting is not only about abstaining from food and drink, it is also about patience, mentioning God, thankfulness, and meditation. Pilgrimage is not only walking or jogging around the Kaaba, going between the two hills of Safa and Marwa and offering the sacrifice, it is also about remembering the Hereafter, uniting with fellow believers, and following the steps of the prophets and messengers.

The level of excellence (*ihsan*) comes next. It involves worshipping God as though you see Him, and (knowing that) while you see Him not yet truly He sees you.

In terms of remembrance, as the Shaykh explained, the level of attentiveness is the level of submission (*islam*), that is, be attentive when you read the Quran or when you mention God. The level of being present with God is the level of belief (*iman*), that is, reflect on the meaning so you feel awe of God. The level of being absent from anything else is the level of excellence (*ihsan*), in which you do not pay attention to what is going around you, but are fully present with God.

We pray to God to elevate us from submission to belief, and from belief to excellence.

NINETEENTH STEP

Calls of distress

The best way to ask Him is through expressing your distress, and the fastest way to acquire good traits is through expressing your humility and need.

IN THE NAME OF GOD, THE LORD OF MERCY, THE GIVER OF MERCY

The words of wisdom discussed here concern *dua* (supplication). It is not about the etiquette of supplication, but the condition of the heart during supplication.

God asks the disbelievers about their own experiences: *Who is it that responds to the distressed when he calls out to Him, and who removes the ill, and has made you inherit the earth? Could there be any divine power besides God?* (Quran 27:62). In this verse God makes it clear to the disbelievers that when they were in distress and sincerely asked God for help, He answered them. If this is the case with disbelievers in distress, what about if a believer is in distress and asks His Lord for help!

Therefore, with distress the supplication is answered quickly. The Shaykh says: "The best way to ask Him is through your distress." If you are in distress and ask God sincerely, while feeling the need for His help after the means have failed you, then rest assured that God will answer your supplication.

This applies not only to asking God for worldly help, but also for help with matters of faith as well. The best way to ask Him to guide you is also through distress, need, humility, and hope in His mercy. This is best illustrated in the Prophet's supplication is different situations.

In the battle of Badr the Prophet ﷺ turned towards the *qibla* (prayer direction), stretched out his arms and began to supplicate his Lord:

"O God, accomplish for me what You have promised me. O God, bring about what You have promised me. O God, if this small band of Muslims is destroyed, you will not be worshipped on this earth after today!" He continued his supplication to God for a long time, until his mantle slipped down from his shoulders.[35] This is a supplication from someone in distress, and it was a supplication that was answered swiftly.

Then the Shaykh explained other useful aspects of supplication. He said, "And the fastest way to acquire good traits is through expressing your humility and need." Some scholars comment on the verse, *charity is for the poor* (Quran 9:60), saying that: If a person gives charity to a poor person in need, what if the poor person shows his need to God? Surely God will give him out of His bounties, even more than what another person might give him.

According to the prophetic traditions we know, the person who performs a supplication should face the *qibla* (prayer direction), stretch out his hand while praying to God, and start the supplication by praising God and invoking peace and blessing on the Prophet. It is also recommended that he invoke peace and blessing on the Prophet in the middle and at the end of the supplication. This is the outward act of supplication. However, what is more important is the condition of the heart when praying to God; this we often neglect even when we follow the Prophet in other ways.

The Prophet used to recite certain prayers in certain situations, such as getting up in the morning, going to bed, getting dressed, taking off his clothes, looking in the mirror, washing himself, sleeping, seeing a new moon, in the evening, in the morning, going out, coming back home, and so on. It is not enough that we follow the Prophet by memorising and uttering these supplications. We must acquire the spirit behind them, which is to be connected with God at all times.

If we trace the history of supplication, we will not find any person, even previous prophets, who made a continuous stream of supplications as much as the Prophet Muhammad did. If we survey the Psalms, the Torah, and the Gospel, we will not come across as many supplications as we find when we study Muhammad's tradition ﷺ.

Moreover, we also learn that the Prophet Muhammad's supplications were accompanied by deep emotions. Aisha, the Prophet's wife, was asked by Ata about the most amazing event she witnessed about the Messenger of God. She cried and said: What was not amazing about him? One night he came and got in bed with me. My skin touched his and he said: "O Abu Bakr's daughter, let me go! Let me worship my Lord." I said: "I love being with you, but I prefer to do as you wish." I let him. He got up and took ablution without wasting water. Then he started praying and crying. He cried so much that his tears flowed down his chest. Then he bent for *ruqu* and cried. Then he prostrated for *sujud* and continued to cry. Then he raised his head and still cried. He continued to cry until morning. When it was time for the dawn prayer (*fajr*), Bilal came and recited the *adhan* (call to prayer). And then I said: "O the Messenger of God! What makes you cry? God has forgiven your sins, those committed and yet to be committed." He said: "Shall I not be a thankful servant to God? Shall I not give Him thanks?"[36]

Prayers may be answered immediately and may be answered later. The Prophet is reported to have said: "A servant will be rewarded on the Day of Judgment for supplications to God, even the ones that were not answered; the reward will be so great that he will wish that his supplications were not answered [in this life]."

When God does not answer your prayers immediately, be certain that God is choosing the best for you. God has always been choosing the best for you. God says about Himself: *In His Hand is all good* (Quran 3:26). And God's giving may be in this world or in the world to come, and the choice is His. *And thus it is: Your Sustainer creates whatever He wills; and He chooses for mankind whatever is best for them* (Quran 26:68).

TWENTIETH STEP

Certainty of faith and indifference about the world

If the light of deep faith shines on you, you will see the Hereafter before journeying to it, and you will see the trappings of this world vanishing before your eyes.

IN THE NAME OF GOD, THE LORD OF MERCY, THE GIVER OF MERCY

The journey to God in this life is much shorter than the journey to Him in the afterlife. One should not forget that death is a reality for all of us. All humans, believers and disbelievers, agree that death is the definite end of this life.

The Prophet ﷺ warned us against striving only for this world. Again, this does not mean that we neglect our worldly affairs under the pretext that we are devoting our life to the Hereafter. What the Prophet meant is that we should not forget the Hereafter.

The Prophet is reported to have said: "Whoever wakes up and this world is his main concern, God will make him scattered and shattered, and he will feel a sense of panic and loss, and he will get nothing of this world except that which was already decreed for him. But whoever gets up and is mostly concerned about the Hereafter, God will cause him to feel focused and content, and will give him a feeling of being independent, and worldly gains will definitely come to him."[37]

When you open your eyes in the morning, ask yourself: What is the first thing that comes to my mind? What is my goal? Is it the Hereafter? Is it about God? If this is the case, God will grant you contentment and cause this worldly life to come to you despite your indifference to it.

By contrast, if you open your eyes thinking of so and so or such and such of worldly matters, even it is lawful, the Prophet says about this person that God will make him scattered and shattered. This means that he will not be satisfied with whatever he gains and achieves. Rather he will always feel that he is still suffering poverty and need, and his greed will be endless.

The question is, how can we reach the level of thinking of the Hereafter? How can we always call it to our minds? The Shaykh links our remembrance of the Hereafter with our certainty of faith. He says that the more our certainty of faith increases, the more we will care about the Hereafter. He sums up this meaning in these words of wisdom: "If the light of deep faith shines on you, you will see the Hereafter before journeying to it, and you will see the trappings of this world vanishing before your eyes."

The Shaykh links certainty of faith to the remembrance of the Hereafter. And how can we reach certainty of faith? The answer comes from the book of God: *and worship your Sustainer till certainty of faith comes to you* (Quran 15:99). The Prophet's Companions experienced this feeling when they studied the Quran and worshipped God. It is reported that one of the Companions said: "When we sit with the Prophet and discuss matters of faith, it is as if we see heaven and hell with our eyes."[38]

Again, this does not mean that we isolate ourselves and renounce this worldly life. This is a wrong understanding that leads to an incorrect practice of the issue of remembering the Hereafter. Indifference about this life does not mean renunciation of the world; it only means to be aware of the afterlife on a spiritual level. This is how balance can be achieved. *Exult not in your wealth, for, verily, God does not love those who exult [in things vain]!—Seek instead, by means of what God has granted you, the good of the life to come, without forgetting your own rightful share in this world; and do good as God has done good to you; and seek not to spread corruption on earth: for, verily, God does not love the spreaders of corruption!* (Quran 28:76–77).

Then, the Shaykh said, "and you will see the trappings of this world vanishing before your eyes." This world is in a continuous state of vanishing. Hasan al-Basri once said: "Son of Adam! You are nothing but a number of days, with each day that passes a part of you is gone."

The Shaykh says that if you have a deep belief in the Hereafter, you will see this world vanishing before your eyes. This will make you indifferent about it and its pleasures, and will draw you nearer to the Hereafter. We are much in need of this proper understanding because we easily forget the Hereafter and do not think about death.

The Prophet ﷺ saw some Companions praising a man because of his good deeds. The Prophet asked them if he used to remember death. They said: We did not hear him mentioning death. Then the Prophet said: "Your friend is not there." This means that he will not reach the high degrees of Paradise because he did not remember death, as remembering death makes one ready for the Hereafter.

Striving for this world only leads to loss in both lives, whereas remembering the Hereafter makes us successful in both lives. *If one desires the rewards of this world, [let him remember that] with God are the rewards of both this world and the life to come: and God is indeed All-Hearing, All-Seeing* (Quran 4:134).

There is no harm in caring for the pleasures of this life. But life should remain in our hands, not in our hearts. This is the correct definition of *zuhd* (indifference about this world), that is, to hold this world and its pleasures in your hand, but not let them into your heart.

TWENTY-FIRST STEP

Dealing with people's praise

When people praise you for what they assume about you, blame yourself for what you know with certainty about yourself. The most ignorant is the one who denies what he really knows about himself and believes what others assume about him.

IN THE NAME OF GOD, THE LORD OF MERCY, THE GIVER OF MERCY

While journeying to God we will be put to many tests. One of those tests pertains to people's praise for what they assume about us. These words of wisdom answer this question, how does one deal with people's praise?

People's praise is a serious danger. A man praised another greatly before the Prophet ﷺ. The Prophet said, "Woe on you! You have cut the neck of your friend." The Prophet repeated this sentence many times and said: "If you have to praise someone, then he should say, 'I think that he is so-and-so,' if he really thinks that he is such. God is the One who will take his accounts, as He knows his reality and no one can sanctify anyone before God."[39]

In another tradition, the Prophet said: "When you see those who shower praise upon others, throw dust upon their faces."[40]

People's praise may change one's intentions from pleasing God to pleasing people, earning their praise, or avoiding their criticism. It also discourages one from doing additional good deeds, if he really believes that he is perfect and has done great actions. Another negative aspect of praise is that it makes one overlook his flaws and, instead, look at his merits.

In these words of wisdom, the Shaykh says: "When people praise you for what they assume about you, blame yourself for what you know with certainty about yourself." People praise based on assumptions and what they know from the external things they see. But we know ourselves and our flaws better than others do.

Remember that the Shaykh said: "Attempting to discover the flaws within you is better than attempting to discover the spiritual worlds hidden from you." Now that you know many of your flaws, when you are highly praised by people, you should turn within and hold yourself accountable for the flaws you know. This will make you pray to God to forgive your sins and help you mend your flaws.

This brings to mind Imam Ali's great speech on the pious ones (may God be pleased be with him). He described the Companions (may God be pleased with them) in a famous sermon, as follows: "If someone praises one of them, he says, 'I know myself better than others, and my Lord is more knowledgeable of me than myself. O God, do not take me to task for what they say, and make me better than what they think of me, and forgive me for those sins which they are unaware of.'"

According to Imam Ali's description, when someone praised one of the Prophet's Companions, he responded to him saying: "I know myself better than others [know me]." This is the same meaning given by Ibn Ata here. The Companion added: "And my Lord is more knowledgeable of me than myself," that is, God is more knowledgeable of my flaws, sins, and mistakes than I am. Finally, the Companion ended his response by praying to God: "Make me better than what they think of me." They think good of me, so make me better than this. "O God, forgive me for those sins which they are unaware of."

Sometimes people's praise takes away the reward promised by God for a certain good deed. Because this praise is actually the reward that one was seeking, as his intention was not to please God, but to please people. This is, by definition, hypocrisy.

The Shaykh said: "If the believer is praised, he should feel ashamed of God that people praise him for things which are not in him. The most ignorant is the one who denies what he really knows about himself and believes what others assume about him." Should I leave what I know with certainty about myself and believe what people assume about me?

In some other cases, people's praise is glad tidings for the believer. Abu Dharr (may God be pleased him) reported: It was said to God's Messenger ﷺ: What is your opinion about the person who has done good deeds and the people praise him? He said: "It is glad tidings for a believer."[41] The Quran mentions the same meaning: *For them there is the glad tiding of happiness in the life of this world and in the life to come* (Quran 10:64).

Thus, a believer should thank God for the difference that people think he makes in their lives. Yet, he should not forget his own flaws.

TWENTY-SECOND STEP

Mercy with people's faults

A person who learns of people's secrets and does not have heavenly mercy on them brings upon himself great danger and disaster.

IN THE NAME OF GOD, THE LORD OF MERCY, THE GIVER OF MERCY

When one's knowledge and awareness increase, he will find himself in situations in which he becomes involved in many social matters, and starts to learn about people's secrets, faults, and problems. This happens when he is consulted about a problem or becomes an arbitrator in certain disputes at the level of the individual, family, or society. Another source of knowledge is experience and insight that one gains over time; this allows one to judge people's nature and real character based on their outward appearance and what is between the lines of their speech or writing.

Learning people's secrets and their weaknesses is a form of power over them. A believer who happens to learn people's secrets should also learn how to deal with them. Here the Shaykh said, "A person who learns of people's secrets and does not have heavenly mercy on them brings upon himself great danger and disaster."

First, one should not feel that he is authorised by God to act as a judge or have any illusion that he is on a great mission to establish justice based on the secrets he came to know.

Second, one must have what the Shaykh called "heavenly mercy" on others involved in the secrets. And heavenly mercy requires that one should not reveal people's faults. God is the One who conceals people's faults. A man called Maiz came to the Prophet confessing that he committed adultery. Hazzal, the Companion, said: "I saw him and ordered him to confess." The Prophet then said, "It would have been better for you if you had covered him with your robe, Hazzal."[42]

It is a major sin to reveal people's faults or use their faults against them. The Prophet is reported to have said: "A believer who conceals the faults of others in this world, God will conceal his faults on the Day of Resurrection."[43]

Third, having heavenly mercy on people also requires that you advise people and call them to do good deeds with a view to correcting their faults. This is how the Prophet behaved with the hypocrites after God told him about what they hid in their hearts. *As for them—God knows all that is in their hearts; so leave them alone, and advise them, and speak unto them about themselves in a gravely searching manner* (Quran 4:64).

When God Himself commands us to do something, His commandments are conveyed in a most gentle way. God says in a hadith qudsi: "If they offer repentance, I will surely love them. If they do not repent, I will be like their physician who helps them with their diseases until they are recovered."

Thus, having heavenly mercy on people also requires that you follow, like a physician, a gradual course in treating people's diseases. A physician also tries different medicines until a certain medicine works out. A good physician resorts to surgery only as the very last option.

Finally, having heavenly mercy on people requires that you free yourself from any personal interest when you handle people's secrets or information which you learn about them. As mentioned earlier, knowing people's secrets gives power over them. An ignorant person might exploit this power for his own interests. This contradicts the concept of heavenly mercy, which urges one to overlook his own interests and aims only at fixing and correcting people's behaviour for their own sake.

A person who does not have mercy on people after learning about their faults, risks falling into tyranny, arrogance, conceit, envy, and suspicion. All these traits are dangerous and destructive, and are punishable both in this world and the world to come. Thus, the

Shaykh said: "A person who learns of people's secrets and does not have heavenly mercy on them brings upon himself great danger and disaster." These words of wisdom are reinforced by the hadith in which the Prophet says: "No sin has a faster divine punishment than the sin of injustice."[44]

The original situation is: *do not spy* (Quran 49:12). But if one finds himself in a situation in which people's secrets are revealed before him, he should have heavenly mercy on them as the Shaykh says. Otherwise, he will be journeying backward not forward to God.

TWENTY-THIRD STEP

Witnessing God's bounty and your shortcomings

To open the doors of hope in Him, recall what He offers you; to open the doors of awe of Him, recall what you offer Him.

IN THE NAME OF GOD, THE LORD OF MERCY, THE GIVER OF MERCY

Sometimes our sins, forgetfulness, and lusts block our way to God, and we do not find an overwhelming longing for Him. Here the Shaykh guides us to two doors that can be opened by reason. Reason is a tool that God granted us and we can use anytime. The two doors are that of hope and awe.

The Shaykh addresses two questions: How can the door of hope be opened while we do not feel this hope in our hearts? How can the door of awe be opened while we do not feel this awe in our hearts?

He replies, try to calculate the bounties that God bestows on you, and calculate the acts of worship and the good deeds that you offer Him.

As for God's bounties, they are innumerable. God says: *For, should you try to count God's blessings, you could never compute them!* (Quran 16:18). When you remember one of God's bounties, you will realise that He is Generous, Merciful, and Most-Forbearing. When we are preoccupied by these meanings, the door of hope in God's generosity, forbearance, and mercy will be opened for us. And when we remember our shortcomings, then the door of awe will be opened in our hearts.

A believer's condition should vary between hope and awe so that he will become, as Ibn al-Qayyim describes, like a bird with two wings; one wing for hope and the other for awe. Striking a balance between opposites is one of the fixed universal laws of God. Here we should strike a balance between hope and awe so that the bird can fly; it cannot fly with one wing.

TWENTY-FOURTH STEP

Keeping priorities straight

A sign of following one's whims is to be active with optional good deeds while being lazy with required obligations.

IN THE NAME OF GOD, THE LORD OF MERCY, THE GIVER OF MERCY

The next step in our journey to God requires sound knowledge and deep understanding. The Prophet ﷺ said: "If God wishes to elevate someone, He grants him knowledge (*fiqh*) of the faith."[45]

Knowledge (*fiqh*) is not only about the judicial rulings pertaining to the practical rituals and social aspects of the faith. In principle, *fiqh* refers to the deep understanding and full comprehension of Islamic law and its different rulings. This deep understanding is very important in our journey to God.

In Islamic law, there are principles (usul) and secondary issues (furu). Principles have priority over secondary issues. There are obligations and optional good deeds. Obligations have priority over optional deeds. There are major sins and minor sins. Avoiding major sins takes priority over avoiding minor sins. The action of the heart is more important than the action of other organs of the body, and thus has a higher priority. The sin committed in the heart is more dangerous than the sin committed by the other organs. And so on. Be aware of those differences and their implications; otherwise, one may be following a whim and not a proper understanding of Islamic law. Without a knowledge of priorities, one may be follow outward appearances aFor example, if you have some money by which you can either perform the pilgrimage or help in improving the building of a mosque, a proper understanding entails that you perform the pilgrimage first. The pilgrimage is an obligation and one of the pillars of Islam, and thus it has to be performed first, whereas improving or beautifying the building of a mosque is optional and in fact not required. If you give priority to the optional deed over the principle obligation then, the Shaykh says, you are following your whim, not the right path.

However, if this money is needed for medication for an elderly parent, for example, then you should spend this money on them and delay the performance of pilgrimage. Taking care of one's parents is an immediate obligation, while pilgrimage is an obligation that can be delayed. Doing the opposite is a sign of following one's whims, not proper knowledge.

Another example can be given: if you have a limited time to perform the obligatory prayer and by performing the two *rakat* (units of prayer) of greeting the mosque you will miss the obligatory prayer, then you should perform the obligatory prayer and give up the greeting prayer. If you perform the prayer for greeting the mosque first and thus miss praying the obligatory prayer during its time, this is a sign of misunderstanding and following whims.

Unfortunately, some people are keen to perform optional good deeds, and especially ritual formalities, while they are careless with basic obligations of the faith. It is agreed that being kind to one's parents is an obligation: *For your Sustainer has ordained that you shall worship none but Him. And do good unto [your] parents. Should one of them, or both, attain to old age in your care, never say "Ugh" to them or scold them, but [always] speak unto them with reverent speech* (Quran 17:23).

It is also obligatory to return the trusts to people: *then let him who is trusted fulfil his trust, and let him be conscious of God* (Quran 2:283). A believer is also required not to curse. The Prophet said: "It is not fitting for a believer to curse or defame (something or someone)."[46]

Unfortunately, in present-day societies and communities, some people claim that they follow the Prophet's way of life, that is, his way of dressing, his outward appearance, his way of sitting, the colour of his clothes, and so forth. Yet, the very same people may mistreat their parents, amass a fortune through corruption, misuse the public trust or resources, or curse and backbite against people. In other words, they fulfill the outward, but miss the obligatory.

Other people may not perform the obligatory prayers, but perform the Eid prayer even under the most difficult circumstances, even though the Eid prayer is optional. This is another example of following one's whims.

Some people commit grave sins in public and even on TV. The same people, ironically, are in the habit of performing *umra* every year! *Umra* is optional, but refraining from spreading mischief is obligatory.

We often hear a hadith in which God speaks about optional good deeds. "And my servant continues to draw near to Me with optional works so that I shall love him. When I love him I am his hearing with which he hears, his seeing with which he sees, his hand with which he strikes and his foot with which he walks."[47] But we forget that "And my servant" is not the beginning of the hadith. The beginning of the hadith, in all of its different narrations, is "My servant draws not near to Me with anything more loved by Me than the duties I have enjoined upon him."

If we perform the obligations such as prayers, *zakah*, fasting, and pilgrimage, giving up sins, being kind to parents, treating the young and the old gently, and so on, we shall enter Paradise. When the Prophet was asked about Islam, he did not begin with the formalities or outward appearances. A Bedouin came to the Prophet and said, "O God's messenger! Inform me what God has made compulsory for me with regard to the prayers." He replied: "You have to offer perfectly the five compulsory prayers in a day and night, unless you want to pray optional prayer."

Here the Prophet did not detail the optional prayer, but he continued to mention the other obligations, as we read in the rest of the tradition.

The Bedouin further asked, "Inform me what God has made compulsory for me with regard to fasting." He replied, "You have to fast during the whole month of Ramadan, unless you want to fast more as optional fasting." The Bedouin further asked, "Tell me how much *zakah* God has enjoined on me." Thus, the Prophet informed him about all the fundamentals of Islam. The Bedouin then said, "By Him who has honoured you, I will not perform any optional deeds nor will I decrease what God has enjoined on me. The Prophet said, "If he is saying the truth, he will succeed and will be granted Paradise."[48]

The Prophet's last words in this hadith imply that if we are sincere with God in performing the obligations without ever performing the optional deeds, we will succeed and be granted Paradise.

We pray to God to grant us correct understanding and sound knowledge so that we will be well guided on our journey to Him.

TWENTY-FIFTH STEP

Telling people about their Lord

Every speech comes out with an aspect that reflects the heart of the speaker. If God allows a speaker to express himself, people will understand his words and comprehend his gestures.

IN THE NAME OF GOD, THE LORD OF MERCY, THE GIVER OF MERCY

This stage on our journey to God relates to the speech in which the believers tell people about God. Every believer has a responsibility to call people to their Creator, to remind them of their Lord, and to participate in reform. *I desire no more than reform in so far as it lies within my power* (Quran 11:88), *Say [O Prophet]: "This is my way: Resting upon conscious insight accessible to reason, I am calling you all unto God—I and they who follow me"* (Quran 12:108). This was the mission of every prophet of God and every follower of the right path.

There are different kinds of speech. There is a certain type of speech that has a considerable influence on people. This speech, as the Shaykh explains, is not the fluent speech that comes from an intelligent mind or an eloquent tongue, rather it is the speech that comes from an enlightened heart.

Recall the many speeches given by prophets, reformers, and righteous leaders; a few sentences that changed the course of history. Their words came from pure hearts. Some of these speeches deserved to be recorded by God in His Glorious Book, the Quran. The following are a few examples.

Here is a speech delivered by Prophet Abraham ﷺ: *Said Abraham: "Have you, then, ever considered what it is that you have been worshipping—*

you and those ancient forebears of yours? Now as for me, I know that, verily, these false deities are my enemies, and that none is my helper save the Sustainer of all the worlds, who has created me and is the One who guides me, and is the One who feeds me and gives me drink, and when I fall ill, is the One who restores me to health, and who will cause me to die and then will bring me back to life, and who, I hope, will forgive me my faults on Judgment Day! O my Sustainer! Endow me with the ability to judge between right and wrong, and make me one with the righteous, and grant me the power to convey the truth unto those who will come after me, and place me among those who will inherit the garden of bliss! And forgive my father for, verily, he is among those who have gone astray, and do not put me to shame on the Day when all will be raised from the dead: and when only he will be happy who comes before God with a heart free of evil!" (Quran 26:75–89).

Read also the speech of Prophet Noah ﷺ: *And convey unto them the story of Noah—when he said unto his people: "O my people! If my presence among you and my announcement of God's messages are repugnant to you—well, in God have I placed my trust. Decide, then, upon what you are going to do against me, and call to your aid those beings to whom you ascribe a share in God's divinity; and once you have chosen your course of action, let no hesitation deflect you from it; and then carry out against me whatever you may have decided, and give me no respite! But if you turn away from the message which I bear, remember that I have asked no reward whatever of you: my reward rests with none but God, for I have been bidden to be among those who have surrendered themselves unto Him"* (Quran 10:71–72).

Read also this dialogue between the Prophet Moses and Pharaoh and his people: *Said Pharaoh: "And what and who is that 'Sustainer of all the worlds'?" Moses answered: "He is the Sustainer of the heavens and the earth and all that is between them: if you would but allow yourselves to be convinced!" Said Pharaoh unto those around him: "Did you hear what he said?" And Moses continued: "He is your Sustainer, too, as well as the Sustainer of your forefathers of old!" Pharaoh exclaimed: "Behold, your 'messenger' who claims that he has been sent unto you is mad indeed! But Moses went on: "He of whom I speak is the Sustainer of the east and the west and of all that is between the two"—as you would know if you would but use your reason!" Said Pharaoh: "Indeed, if you choose to worship any deity other than me, I shall most cer-*

tainly throw you into prison!" Said he: "Even if I should bring about before you something that clearly shows the truth?" (Quran 26:22–30).

Read also the speech of the Prophet Jesus ﷺ: *But Jesus said: "Behold, I am a servant of God. He has vouchsafed unto me revelation and made me a prophet, and made me blessed wherever I may be; and He has enjoined upon me prayer and charity as long as I live, and has endowed me with piety towards my mother; and He has not made me haughty or bereft of grace. Hence, peace was upon me on the day when I was born, and will be upon me on the day of my death, and on the day when I shall be raised to life again!"* (Quran 19:30-33).

Read the speech of the believing man of Pharaoh's family: "*The man who believed said further: "O my people! Follow me: I will lead you to the Path of Right. O my people! This life of the present is nothing but (temporary) convenience: It is the Hereafter that is the Home that will last. He that works evil will not be requited but by the like thereof: and he that works a righteous deed - whether man or woman - and is a Believer- such will enter the Garden (of Bliss): Therein will they have abundance without measure. And O my people! How (strange) it is for me to call you to Salvation while ye call me to the Fire! You do call upon me to blaspheme against God, and to join with Him partners of whom I have no knowledge; and I call you to the Exalted in Power, Who forgives again and again! Without doubt you do call me to one who is not fit to be called to, whether in this world, or in the Hereafter; our return will be to God. and the Transgressors will be Companions of the Fire! Soon will you remember what I say to you (now), My (own) affair I commit to God. for God (ever) watches over His Servants.""* (Quran 40:38–44)

You can feel, through the words, that all these speeches had aspects of light shining through from the hearts of the speakers.

The same holds true for the Prophet Muhammad's speech. Read, for example, his speech in the battle of Tabuk:

"Verily the most veracious discourse is the book of God. The most trustworthy handhold is the word of piety. The best of religions is the religion of Abraham. The best of traditions is the Sunna of Muhammad. The noblest speech is the mentioning of God. The finest of narratives is this Quran. The best of affairs is that which has been firmly resolved upon. The worst matters are those which are created without heavenly sanction. The best of ways is the one trodden by the prophets. The noblest death is the death of a martyr. The most miserable blindness is waywardness after guidance. The best of knowledge is that which is beneficent. The best guidance is that which is put into practice. The worst blindness is the blindness of the heart. The upper hand is better than the lower (that is, it is better to give than to receive). The little that suffices is better than the abundant and alluring. The worst apology is that which is tendered when death stares one in the face. The worst remorse is that which is felt on the Day of Resurrection. Some men do not come to the Friday prayer, but with hesitance and delay. And some of them do not remember God but with reluctance. The tongue that is addicted to false expression is a bubbling spring of sins. The most valuable possession is contentment of the heart. The best provision is that of piety. The highest wisdom is the awe of God. The best thing to be cherished in the hearts is faith and conviction; doubt is part of infidelity. Impatient wailing and fulsome praise of the dead is an act of ignorance. Betrayal leads one to the fire of hell. Liquor is the mother of evils. Each one of you must resort to a place of four cubits (in the grave). Your affairs will be decided ultimately in the next life. He who pardons is himself granted pardon. He who forgives others, is forgiven by God. He who represses anger, God rewards him. He who faces misfortunes with perseverance, God compensates him. He who shows patience and forbearance, God doubles his reward. He who disobeys God, God chastises him."[49]

This is a speech from the Prophet's heart that reached the people easily and had a considerable influence on them. Anyone who tells the people about their Creator must first ensure that his speech arises from the heart.

If you want to offer advice to anyone, mend your heart first. When you have a sincere intention in your heart, your influence on people will be stronger, that is, people will understand your words and comprehend your gestures, as the Shaykh says in these words of wisdom.

The Prophet's Companions also gave eloquent speeches that not only influenced their audiences but also changed the course of history. Abu Bakr al-Siddiq (may God be pleased with him) gave a very important speech immediately after he became caliph. One of the most influential statements was the following: "I have been given the authority over you, and I am not the best of you. If I do well, help me; and if I do wrong, set me right."

Umar b. al-Khattab (may God be pleased with him) said: "When did you enslave people whose mothers bore them free?" Uthman b. Affan (may God be pleased with him) said: "O people, you need a ruler who is a good doer not a ruler who is a good speaker." Ali b. Abi Talib (may God be pleased with him) said: "The keeper of a safe dies and what he guards and the treasures remain, however, a man of knowledge lives throughout the ages."

Ibn Ata is right: If God allows a speaker to express himself, people will understand his words and comprehend his gestures.

TWENTY-SIXTH STEP

Satisfaction

His most perfect blessing on you is to give you just enough, and to deprive you of what will cause you to do wrong. When you have less to be happy with, you will have less to be sad about.

IN THE NAME OF GOD, THE LORD OF MERCY, THE GIVER OF MERCY

This stage of our journey to God relates to the issue of providence and how to understand it correctly. The prophetic hadith, mentioned above, that says: "The little that suffices is better than the abundant and alluring," has been reworded by the Shaykh in these words of wisdom. The Shaykh says: "His most perfect blessing on you is to give you just enough, and to deprive you of what will cause you to do wrong."

God may give a believer just enough, not more or less. When this happens, it is a perfect blessing from God. If God gives abundant providence to someone, there is a risk of that person transgressing boundaries. God says: *Nay, but a human does transgress all bounds. Is it because he looks upon himself as self-sufficient? Verily, to your Lord is the return of all* (Quran 96:6).

In the following verse God tells us about human nature: *For, if God were to grant in this world abundant sustenance to His servants, they would behave on earth in transgression and rebellion beyond all bounds: but as it is, He bestows His grace from on high in due measure, as He wills* (Quran 42:27). This is a universal law pertaining to human nature; if God grants us abundant providence, we will do wrong. Thus, God *bestows His grace from on high in due measure, as He wills* (Quran 42:27).

God, in His infinite knowledge, knows that if He gives a certain person wealth, that person will not do wrong. So, He gives him wealth. At the same time, He knows that if He gives him power, he will do injustice to people. Therefore, God does not grant him power. And vice versa.

This applies to different kinds of giving and depriving. Whatever you are given is from God's bounties and He is protecting you, even from yourself. So, do not look only at what you are deprived of and wish to get something that might cause you to do wrong because "the little that suffices is better than the abundant and alluring," as the Prophet ﷺ said.

Then the Shaykh says: "When you have less to be happy with, you will have less to be sad about." Feeling joyful is not denounced in Islam. God says: *Say: "In bounty of God and in His grace—in this, then, let them rejoice* (Quran 10:58). A believer feels happy for the bounties that God bestows on him. However, feeling miserable for what is missed is not the right response. God says: *Know this, so that you may not despair over whatever good has escaped you nor exult unduly over whatever good has come to you* (Quran 57:23).

If you feel happy for worldly gains, know that this life will come to an end. There is an Arabic statement: If what you have had lasted with the person before you, it would not have reached you! God says: *All that lives on earth or in the heavens is bound to pass away* (Quran 55:26).

Thus, if you have less to be happy with, then there will be less to be sad about. It is out of God's bounty that He gives you just enough, so that you will not be sad for missing things you do not need. If you have enough food, drink, and providence, this is a perfect blessing from God and you should thank God for that. God has a perfect wisdom in giving and depriving; He wants the best for you, be satisfied with that.

TWENTY-SEVENTH STEP

Humbleness

A person is not humble if he thinks that he is above his act of humbleness. A humble person thinks he is below his act of humbleness.

IN THE NAME OF GOD, THE LORD OF MERCY, THE GIVER OF MERCY

Humbleness is a basic trait of those journeying to God and a characteristic that every servant should be keen on maintaining. Arrogance is the opposite of humbleness and is a serious flaw, as discussed before. The Prophet ﷺ said: "He who has in his heart the weight of a mustard seed of arrogance shall not enter Paradise." The Companions said: "But a man likes to wear a nice robe and nice sandals." The Prophet replied: "This is not arrogance. Arrogance is denying the truth and injustice to people."[50]

God says: *"And turn not your cheek away from people in false pride, and walk not haughtily on earth: for, behold, God does not love anyone who, out of conceit, acts in a boastful manner* (Quran 31:18), and *as for that happy life in the hereafter, We grant it only to those who do not seek to exalt themselves on earth, nor yet to spread corruption* (Quran 28:83).

Some people behave humbly with others, but at the same time, they think and feel that they are superior to them! This is arrogance and has nothing to do with humbleness. Humbleness should come from the heart. The Shaykh explains that a person who is humble with others thinks that he is indeed inferior to them.

The question is, how does one reach that feeling of humbleness? The Shaykh answers, by considering faith. Perhaps someone is clearly inferior in terms of position or wealth, however, if faith is a criteria for status, perhaps he is much closer to God than others, or his belief is much stronger. Perhaps he is afflicted with real trials in this life and he is enduring them patiently and wisely for the sake of God. He could very well be better than others in the sight of God.

Sahl al-Saidi narrated that: A man passed by the Prophet and the Prophet asked his Companions: "What do you say about this man?" They replied: "If he asks for a woman's hand, he ought to be given her in marriage; and if he intercedes for someone, his intercession should be accepted; and if he speaks, he should be listened to." The Prophet kept silent, and then a man from among the poor Muslims passed by, and the Prophet asked them: "What do you say about this man?" They replied: "If he asks for a woman's hand in marriage he does not deserve to be married, and he intercedes for someone, his intercession should not be accepted; and if he speaks, he should not be listened to." The Prophet said, "This poor man is better than the earth's fill of the first man."[51]

The first evaluation given by the Companions was based on material standards. The real evaluation considers the criterion of faith alone, and this what the Prophet applied. The second man, in terms of faith, is better than billions of the likes of the first man.

Real humbleness is to see yourself as inferior to others because piety is the criterion for status and nobility, according to the Quran. *Verily, the noblest of you in the sight of God is the one who is most pious* (Quran 49:13). And this criterion is known only to God, *He knows best as to who is pious* (Quran 53:32).

A humble person, the Shaykh says, is not the one who thinks that he is above his act of humbleness. A humble person is the one who thinks he is below his act of humbleness.

Look at the example of the Prophet who was ordered by God to *spread the wings of your tenderness over the believers* (Quran 15:88). Spreading the wings of tenderness is the same expression that God used for the attitude of a believer with his parents. *And spread over them humbly the wings of tenderness* (Quran 17:24). This is the highest rank of humbleness.

God also commanded the Prophet: *Pardon them, then, and pray that they be forgiven, and take counsel with them in all matters of public concern* (Quran 3:159). These are the characteristics of a humble leader; he pardons people, prays that they will be forgiven, and consults them. Anyone who thinks that he does not need people's consultation, or does not need to learn because he knows and understands everything is not humble; rather, he is arrogant. We seek refuge in God from arrogance.

A clear evidence of the Prophet's humbleness can be seen in the way he consulted his Companions on community affairs and changed his opinion accordingly. At the battle of Badr, the Prophet wanted to camp in a certain place. One of the Companions wanted to propose another place for camping. The Companion, al-Habbab, asked, "O Messenger of God, is your opinion based on a revelation from God, or is it a war tactic and strategy?" The Prophet replied: "No, it is a war tactic and strategy." So al-Habbab proposed, "Then this is not the most strategic place to camp." The Prophet Muhammad accepted his advice.

Salman, the Persian Companion of the Prophet, suggested digging a trench to defend Medina from attack and the Prophet applied his idea.

God created us differently in terms of reason, position, health, wealth, and so on. But having one or more of these traits is not a reason for arrogance. In fact, one should be grateful to God if he is blessed with God's blessings. This is an act of worship by the heart. A humble person is not the one who shows his humbleness in front of people or feels in his own heart that his status is above his act of humbleness. A truly humble person is the one who feels that he is inferior to people and that he needs them, their advice, and their prayers for him.

TWENTY-EIGHTH STEP

A blessed life and a continuous impact

How often has a long life brought about so little, and how often has a short life brought about so much. If someone's life is blessed, he will reach, in a short time, bounties from God that cannot be expressed in words or comprehended in descriptions.

IN THE NAME OF GOD, THE LORD OF MERCY, THE GIVER OF MERCY

In Islamic terminology, especially in Sufism, much attention is given to what is called *baraka* (blessing). Blessing is defined as the divine good displayed in something. When we invoke God's blessing in something, it is to bring about favourable results from the divine blessing.

The Shaykh said in these words of wisdom: "How often has a long life brought about so little, and how often has a short life brought about so much." Someone may live for many years without blessing in his life, and another person may live for a short time with much blessing and great good in his life.

Then, the Shaykh said, "If someone's life is blessed, he will reach, in a short time, bounties from God that cannot be expressed in words or comprehended in descriptions." God's bounties in a blessed life are innumerable, even if it is short.

We have a good example in the Prophet Muhammad's life. During the twenty years which he lived after receiving God's revelation, he conveyed God's message to the world, and he changed the course of human history until the Day of Judgment. The Prophet's life was a blessed life that brought about much good and success to all people of all ages in all aspects of life.

Some of the Prophet's Companions died in their thirties and forties, but they contributed greatly to the faith. Musab b. Umayr, for example, died in his twenties, but he served the cause of *dawa* (the call to faith) in Medina before the Prophet's immigration. Abu Bakr al-Siddiq ruled the Muslims for three years only, but he founded a strong state and protected Islam against its many enemies at that time.

Many imams and scholars, such as, al-Shafii, Abu Hamid al-Ghazali, and Ibn Qayyim al-Jawziyya, died in their fifties. Yet they left behind dozens of influential books and thousands of students. Today many centuries after their passing away, their knowledge and wisdom still benefits millions of people every day.

Because God knows that we are far behind these great people, He placed His blessings (*baraka*) in certain times and places. For example, God filled the Night of Destiny with infinite blessings: *We have indeed revealed this (Message) in the Night of Power: And what will explain to you what the Night of Power is? The Night of Power is better than a thousand months. Therein come down the angels and the Spirit by God's permission, on every errand; Peace! This until the rise of morn!* (Quran 97:1–5). Worshipping God in this night is better than worshipping Him for a thousand months other than this night.

God also made Friday a blessed day. The hour before the dawn is a blessed hour. The early hours of the day are blessed by God. If you get up early, everything you do will be blessed, be it work, worship, sports, or anything else.

God has also chosen some places to be more blessed than others. God says: *Limitless in His glory is He who transported His servant by night from the inviolable House of Worship at Mecca to the remote House of Worship at Jerusalem—the environs of which We had blessed* (Quran 17:1)· *Behold, the first house ever set up for mankind was indeed the one at Bakka [Mecca]: rich in blessing, and a source of guidance unto all the worlds* (Quran 3:96).[52] These places have been blessed by God in a special way.

There is abundant blessing (*baraka*) in sincerity. When something is done with pure sincerity for God, it will certainly be blessed. A sincere life is a blessed life that cannot be expressed in words or comprehended in descriptions.

CONCLUSION

Re-starting the journey

What a failure to be free of distractions and not turn back to Him! Or to have fewer obstacles and not journey back to Him!

IN THE NAME OF GOD, THE LORD OF MERCY, THE GIVER OF MERCY

The journey to God does not have an end! It is like a circular road. If you think that you reached the end, it takes you back to where you started. The journey to God is like walking around the Kaaba. These cycles around the Kaaba are manifestations of the universal laws of God. Life on this earth is a cycle that contains many intertwined cycles.

The human cycle starts when the sperm is formed and lasts until one reaches maturity, then a person dies and God raises him again in a different cycle: *Now, indeed, We create a human out of the essence of clay, and then We cause him to remain as a drop of sperm in the wombs firm keeping, and then We create out of the drop of sperm a germ-cell, and then We create out of the germ-cell an embryonic lump, and then We create within the embryonic lump bones, and then We clothe the bones with flesh—and then We bring all this into being as a new creation: hallowed, therefore, is God, the best of creators! And then, behold! after all this, you are destined to die; and then, behold! you shall be raised from the dead on Resurrection Day* (Quran 23:12–16).

A plant's cycle on earth also has the same course as that of the human cycle: *And He it is who sends forth the winds as a glad tiding of His coming grace so that when they have brought heavy clouds, We may drive them towards dead land and cause thereby water to descend; and by this means do We cause all manner of fruit to come forth. Even thus shall We cause the dead to come forth: and this you ought to keep in mind* (Quran 7:57).

The same law of cycles applies to the planets, the moon, and the stars: *He it is who has made the sun a source of radiant light and the moon a light reflected, and has determined for it phases so that you might know how to compute the years and to measure time. None of this has God created without an inner truth. Clearly does He spell out these messages unto people of innate knowledge* (Quran 10:5).

The moon is first born, then it grows and grows until it looks like a complete circle. Then it wanes until it begins a new cycle: *And in the moon, for which We have determined phases which it must traverse till it becomes like an old date-stalk, dried-up and curved. And neither may the sun overtake the moon, nor can the night usurp the time of day, since all of them float through space* (Quran 36:39–40).

Communities and civilizations go through the same cycle—birth, maturity, and death: *for it is by turns that We apportion unto people such days of fortune and misfortune* (Quran 3:140).

The journey to God does not stop. In each stage of one's life, one continues to journey to God in some capacity and at some stage. But at certain stages one becomes less occupied than at other stages. The Shaykh draws our attention to this at the end of his guidelines, by saying: "What a failure to be free of distractions and not turn back to Him! Or to have fewer obstacles and not journey back to Him." This is supported by God's command to the Prophet: *Hence, when you are freed from distress, remain steadfast, and unto your Sustainer turn with love* (Quran 94:7–8).

A believer must make use of free time to re-start the journey. The Prophet ﷺ said: "*Take benefit of five before five: your youth before your old age, your health before your sickness, your wealth before your poverty, your free time before your preoccupation, and your life before your death.*"[53]

As we started the journey putting our hope in God, "If you find yourself having less hope in God when you make a mistake, then realise you are only relying on your work," we end the journey by praying to God to forgive our sins, flaws, and shortcomings. We pray to Him to reward us out of His mercy and grace not because of our work.

We must renew our aspiration, but we have to know that "people's will, however strong it is, can never pierce through the veils of destiny." One must work hard and leave the result to God. "Save yourself from worrying. Someone else already took care of your affairs for you."

We must remind ourselves of sincerity. "Deeds are like statues that only come to life with the spirit of sincerity." We must also remind ourselves that the best course of mending the heart is through reflection in isolation. "There is nothing more beneficial to the heart than isolation that allows it to enter a state of reflection."

In isolation, there is no space for desire and forgetfulness. "How can the mirror of the heart shine if material images cover it? How can the heart journey to God if it is chained by its desires? How can the heart ever hope to enter the divine presence if it has not purified itself from its forgetfulness? How can the heart hope to understand the subtle secrets while not having repented from mistakes?" Indeed, the worship of reflection is the key of excellence.

Every believer should make the best use of his time and life. "Postponing good deeds until you have free time is an indication of an immature soul." One should hasten to do good deeds and refer to God in the beginnings. "A sign of success in the end is to refer to God in the beginning. If there is no sunrise in the beginning, there is no sunrise in the end." This reminds us to purify our intentions, show sincerity, seek God's help, and refer to Him at the start of each act.

Discovering one's flaws does not stop until one eliminates all flaws and acquires good morals. "Trying to discover the flaws within you is better than trying to discover the worlds hidden from you." This is, by nature, an on going process.

The first flaw is to feel self-righteous because, "The origin of every sin, forgetfulness, and lust is in being self-righteous, and the origin of every good deed, awareness, and chastity is in being self-critical." The inner self that tries to discover its flaws is the self-reproaching soul that can be attained if one befriends good people. "Do not befriend someone who does not elevate you with his state, or guide you to God with his speech. It could be that you are doing evil, yet you think that you are doing good, because you are comparing yourself to your friend who is worse than you." So, you have to befriend those who are better than you in terms of righteousness.

Do not stop mentioning God's names because your heart is not present. "Forgetting Him completely is worse than being inattentive while you are mentioning Him; perhaps He will elevate you from being inattentive to being attentive, and from being attentive to being fully present with Him, and from being fully present with Him to being fully absent from anything but Him. *This is not difficult for God* (Quran 35:17).

Another serious flaw is neediness, which leads one to a state of humiliation and servitude to other than God. "The tree of humiliation stems from a seed of neediness. Nothing deceives you as your illusion. You are free from what you gave up, and you are a slave to what you are in need of." Illusion leads us to think that people decide our providence. Always ask for God's providence only, because God is the One in whose hand everything rests. Thus, you feel humiliated before Him, and the real freedom is to be a slave only to God.

"And if you do not advance towards Him by doing excellent deeds, He will pull you towards Him with the chain of tests." The meaning of these words of wisdom is supported by this verse: *And, indeed, We tested them through suffering, but they did not abase themselves before their Sustainer; and they will never humble themselves* (Quran 23:76). "You risk losing your blessings when you do not thank Him for them, and you tie them to you firmly when you do." This meaning is supported by this verse: *If you are grateful to Me, I shall most certainly give you more and more; but if you are ungrateful, verily, My chastisement will be severe indeed!"'* (Quran 14:7).

We must understand God's wisdom in giving and depriving. "You might think that He is giving you, while in reality He is depriving you. And you might think that He is depriving you, while in reality He is giving you." This meaning is supported by this verse: *But as for man, whenever his Sustainer tries him by His generosity and by letting him enjoy a life of ease, he says, "My Sustainer has been generous towards me"; whereas, whenever He tries him by tightening his means of livelihood, he says,*

"My Sustainer has disgraced me!" But nay (Quran 89:15–17).

"You feel bad about your deprivation because you do not understand. He might open the door of worship for you, but does not open the door of acceptance. And you might be destined to sin, but this becomes a means to ascension towards Him. A sin that produces humbleness and need is better than an act of worship that produces arrogance and prejudice."

"If He takes you away from people, then know that He is opening to you the doors of His company." This is not deprivation, because taking you away from people in isolation or travel is a gift from God, not a test.

Supplication should not stop. "And if He allows you to ask, then know that He wants to give you something." The supplication may be answered in this world or the world to come.

"God diversified the acts of worship for you because He knows how quickly you become weary. And He did not permit you certain acts of worship at certain times so you do not go to extremes." To avoid feeling weary, you can diversify the acts of worship; perform prayer, give in charity, fast, or become involved in the many acts of worship that the Prophet showed us.

But all these acts of worship have levels of performance. "Not every performer of prayer perfects them." The levels of humbleness are humiliation followed by reverence followed by joy; that is, submission (*islam*), belief (*iman*), and excellence (*ihsan*).

Then, "The best way to ask Him is through your distress, and the fastest way to acquire good traits is through expressing your humility and need." This meaning is supported by the verse: *Nay—who is it that responds to the distressed when he calls out to Him* (Quran 27:62).

"If the light of deep faith shines on you, you will see the Hereafter before journeying to it, and you will see the trappings of this world vanishing before your eyes." Forgetting death is a serious flaw that every Muslim should remedy. A true believer is the one who always remembers the afterlife.

When a believer is praised by people, he should be careful. "When people praise you for what they assume about you, blame yourself for what you know with certainty about yourself. The most ignorant is the one who denies what he really knows about himself and believes what others assume about him."

It is important to balance hope and fear so that hope does not become a feeling of security from God's punishment. "If you want the doors of hope opened, recall what He offers you, and if you want the doors of awe opened, recall what you offer Him."

"A sign of following one's whims is to be active with optional good deeds while being lazy with required obligations." A true believer should set his priorities aright. He should first perform the obligations, then the optional good deeds. He should use his wealth, effort, and time in carrying out the most essential obligations first.

"Every speech comes out with an aspect that reflects the heart of the speaker. If God allows a speaker to express himself, people will understand his words and comprehend his gestures." The Prophet's comprehensive words changed the world because they came from a pure heart full of light.

Satisfaction is a treasure that is never exhausted because "the little that suffices is better than the abundant and alluring," as the Prophet ﷺ said. "His most perfect blessing on you is to give you just enough, and to deprive you of what will cause you to do wrong. When you have less to be happy with, you will have less to be sad about." This meaning is supported by this verse: *Know this, so that you may not despair over whatever good has escaped you, nor exult unduly over whatever good has come to you* (Quran 57:23).

Humbleness is also a treasure. But, "A person is not humble if he thinks that he is above his act of humbleness. A humble person thinks he is below his act of humbleness."

Finally, the best thing that God grants you is a blessed life. "How often has a long life brought about so little, and how often has a short life brought about so much. If someone's life is blessed, he will reach, in a short time, bounties from God that cannot be expressed in words or comprehended in descriptions." Blessings can also be found in certain places, times and in a pure intention.

Reforming our manners with God will lead to reforming our

manners with people. This is one of God's universal laws of change. *Verily, God does not change a people's condition unless they change their inner selves* (Quran 13:11).

We pray to God to accept these humble words and not to take us for account because of them on the Day of Judgment. We pray to Him to help people make the best use of these words.

O God! Benefit us by that which you have taught us and teach us that which will benefit us and increase us in knowledge. O God, send peace and blessings upon the Prophet Muhammad, his family, his Companions, and whoever follows his guidance until the Last Day.

ENDNOTES

1 My translations of the meanings of the Holy Quran are based on Muhammad Asad's excellent translation, with some modifications to suit the context of this book. In some cases, I use modern words in place of old English, or make substitutions that are closer to the meanings referred to in this text.

2 Reported by al-Bukhari and Muslim.

3 I would like to thank Brother Mohsen Haredy, for his help with the translation and hadith authentication of the Arabic book, which I benefited from in this English version.

4 Reported by Ibn Hibban and Ibn Maja.

5 Reported by Ibn Maja.

6 Reported by al-Tirmidhi.

7 Reported by al-Bukhari and Muslim.

8 Reported by al-Bukhari and Muslim.

9 Reported by al-Bayhaqi.

10 Reported by al-Bukhari and Muslim.

11 Reported by al-Bayhaqi.

12 Reported by al-Bukhari.

13 Reported by al-Bukhari and Muslim.

14 Reported by Ibn Hibban.

15 Reported by al Nasai.

16 Reported by al-Bukhari and Muslim.

17 Reported by al-Bukhari and Muslim.

18 Reported by al-Bayhaqi.

19 Reported by al-Bukhari and Muslim.

20 Reported by al-Tabarani.

21 Reported by al-Bukhari and Muslim.
22 Reported by Ibn Hibban and al-Tirmidhi.
23 Reported by Ibn Hibban and al-Nasai.
24 Reported by al-Nasai.
25 Reported by al-Bukhari.
26 Reported by Muslim.
27 Reported by al-Tirmidhi and Ibn Maja.
28 Reported by al-Tirmidhi.
29 Reported by al-Tirmidhi.
30 Reported by al-Tirmidhi.
31 Reported by al-Tirmidhi.
32 Reported by Abu Dawud.
33 Reported by al-Bukhari.
34 Reported by Muslim.
35 Reported by Muslim.
36 Reported by al-Bukhari.
37 Reported by al-Tirmidhi.
38 Reported by Ibn Maja.
39 Reported by al-Bukhari.
40 Reported by Muslim.
41 Reported by Muslim.
42 Reported by Abu Dawud.
43 Reported by Muslim.
44 Reported in *Musnad* Abi Hanifa
45 Reported by al-Bukhari.
46 Reported by al-Bukhari in his *al-Adab al-mufrad*.
47 Reported by al-Bukhari.
48 Reported by al-Bukhari.
49 Reported by al-Bayhaqi.

50 Reported by Muslim.

51 Reported by Muslim.

52 Quran 3:96, trans. M. Asad.

53 Reported by al-Hakim and al-Bayhaqi.